PRAISE FOR *REL*

School leaders and educators have an opportunity to learn from the lessons of COVID-19 and the movement for racial justice and create schools that fundamentally dismantle the inequities that have been laid bare. This book offers educators essential guidance for transforming their schools in ways that intentionally meet the needs of every student.

—**Nancy Gutierrez**, President, The Leadership Academy

Rebound is a valuable and timely book. This masterful collection of proven strategies to accelerate learning for all students and staff is essential for all school districts. The information provides immediate opportunities for your team and students to achieve maximum impact in teaching and learning as we move forward from distance learning.

—**Martinrex Kedziora**, Superintendent, Moreno Valley Unified School District

Some books come along at exactly the right moment. Arriving just as we begin to heal from our collective trauma, this book provides a combination of inspiration, advice, and practical tools that teachers, leaders, and educational practitioners need to rethink, reimagine, and reinvent the schools our students, families, and educators need and deserve.

—**Sandi Everlove**, Director of Instructional Design, Committee for Children

This book is phenomenal! I really haven't enjoyed reading a practitioner book more in a long time. The way that the authors have structured the book provides a great way for readers to engage and make applications to their own practice. The modules are constructed in an easy-to-use format. There isn't wasted space in this playbook. It's holistic and it addresses such a broad range of topics that it will stand the test of time for educators and administrators who are invested in being better for their school communities.

—**Doug Anthony**, Chief Consultant, Anthony Consulting Group
Former Associate Superintendent of Talent Development
Prince George's County Public Schools

This playbook is for all educators and provides all the elements to ensure we come out of the pandemic on top. From educator self-care to building successful learning systems to meet the needs of each and every student, *Rebound* provides us a clear path to navigate these uncharted waters.

—**Guido Magliato,** Assistant Superintendent, Leadership and Learning
La Mesa-Spring Valley Schools

Rebound is a gift to educators. The book is an amazing resource for all of us to rethink our classrooms and schools as we work to recover from the COVID-19 pandemic. We have had many struggles in education during this pandemic; however, we have also learned new strategies that we need to capture and continue to implement as we move out of the pandemic. This book will help you do that!

—**Debra Kubin,** Superintendent, Ukiah Unified School District

Grades K-12

REBOUND

Grades K-12

REBOUND

A PLAYBOOK FOR REBUILDING AGENCY, ACCELERATING LEARNING RECOVERY, AND RETHINKING SCHOOLS

DOUGLAS FISHER
NANCY FREY
DOMINIQUE SMITH
JOHN HATTIE

FOR INFORMATION:

Corwin

A SAGE Company

2455 Teller Road

Thousand Oaks, California 91320

(800) 233-9936

www.corwin.com

SAGE Publications Ltd.

1 Oliver's Yard

55 City Road

London EC1Y 1SP

United Kingdom

SAGE Publications India Pvt. Ltd.

B 1/I 1 Mohan Cooperative Industrial Area

Mathura Road, New Delhi 110 044

India

SAGE Publications Asia-Pacific Pte. Ltd.

18 Cross Street #10-10/11/12

China Square Central

Singapore 048423

President: Mike Soules

Associate Vice President
  and Editorial Director: Monica Eckman

Director and Publisher, Corwin Classroom: Lisa Luedeke

Editorial Development Manager: Julie Nemer

Associate Content Development Editor: Sharon Wu

Consulting Editor: Sara Johnson

Production Editor: Melanie Birdsall

Copy Editor: Diane DiMura

Typesetter: C&M Digitals (P) Ltd.

Proofreader: Theresa Kay

Indexer: Sheila Hill

Cover and Interior Designer: Gail Buschman

Marketing Manager: Deena Meyer

Image credits:
Module 1: iStock.com/Staras
Module 2: Roman Samborskyi/Shutterstock.com
Module 3: lzf/Shutterstock.com
Module 4: iStock.com/Pekic
Module 5: Ekateryna Zubal/Shutterstock.com
Module 6: Violanda/Shutterstock.com
Module 7: iStock.com/Bogdanhoda
Module 8: Prostock-studio/Shutterstock.com

Printed in the United States of America

Library of Congress Control Number: 2021902115

ISBN 978-1-0718-4889-0

This book is printed on acid-free paper.

21 22 23 24 25 10 9 8 7 6 5 4 3 2

CONTENTS

REBOUND

Something unexpected
Something we've never encountered
Something new to the world
It was quick and fast
With no warning
Everything has now changed
Your life has now changed
It won't ever be the same
We are now lost
What to do next
With no clues
What's the next move?
To Stay Home
Is what we're told
The world is at a standstill
While time continues
Our education must continue
The world in such panic
But we must continue
Scared to step outside
But we must continue
We are the next generation
So we must continue
Time for something new
Something we're not used to
Something so complicated
Yet so simple
We had to adapt
With no other choice
We met a new way
A new way to find knowledge
A new way to learn
The only way left to learn
It was not easy
There were many setbacks
Many failures
Many distractions
Nothing to keep us motivated but Ourselves
A rough beginning
Coming to a peaceful end
Though it's not over

Be proud
Though you may not see
Though you may not understand
This moment is a moment to be proud of
Overcoming the challenge
Pushing through the rain
The light just over the horizon
We're Almost there
We had every chance to give up
Nobody around to tell us this and that
Nobody around to direct us
Nobody around to watch
There is no coming back from this moment
You have now adapted to a new way of learning
You have now adapted to a new way of life
You miss the old way
But this moment has forever helped your future
See it or not
You have been a part of virtual learning
It came unexpectedly
But we picked up right where we left off
We adapt
We continue
We push through
And we make it out
We are the next generation
We have not failed
We have thrived
We took this lesson
And created a blessing
The set up for failure
Has become our greatest success
Entertainers
Entrepreneurs
Hustlers
Is what we have become in a short period of time
With this dark moment, a small light was all we needed
To find our path
They took a shot and missed
We took the rebound and scored

—Jiovanni Gutierrez Montano
Class of 2019–2020
Health Sciences High

ACKNOWLEDGMENTS

Corwin gratefully acknowledges the contributions of the following reviewers:

Doug Anthony
Former Associate Superintendent of Talent Development
Prince George's County Public Schools
Chief Consultant, Anthony Consulting Group

Sandi Everlove
Director of Instructional Design
Committee for Children

Nancy Gutierrez
Executive Director
The Leadership Academy

Sara Johnson
Educational Consultant, Aliso Viejo, CA

Martinrex Kedziora
Superintendent
Moreno Valley Unified School District

Debra Kubin
Superintendent
Ukiah Unified School District

Farrah Lin
Parent, San Diego, CA

Guido Magliato
Assistant Superintendent, Leadership & Learning
La Mesa-Spring Valley Schools

Hilda Maldonado
Superintendent
Santa Barbara Unified School District

Hilda Martinez
Teacher and RTI Coordinator
Zamorano Elementary School, San Diego, CA

INTRODUCTION

You have been stretched. You have been pulled. You have been through the wringer, tested, and tested again. You probably feel like a rubber band, holding it together but under a lot of tension. But the problem with the rubber band analogy is this: They either break or they go back to their former shape. Neither are good options for you, your family, or your students. We need to see and feel the excitement of learning again. We need to engage with our colleagues again. But we also need to heal from the traumatic experiences that have shaped the recent past.

It's time to rebound. We chose this word because it allows us to acknowledge that there will always be an impact from the experiences we've had. There will be a lasting effect from the time we quarantined and were isolated. There will be a lasting impact from seeing some of our students and colleagues suffer. We may have suffered. We have been changed.

But the word *rebound* also acknowledges that there can be increasing value and strength following a decline, setback, or adversity. There is a bounce-back notion contained within the word *rebound*. Rebound asks us to consider what worked well, what did not, what we need to preserve from the prequarantine, and what we need to cherish during quarantine teaching. Rebound means we can go back to the pre-COVID world, or we can learn from it and create better. After all, why would we want to go back to inequitable school systems when we can build something different? We use the term *rebound* in the sense of "our health is on the rebound." That is, we can learn from pandemic teaching to come back better.

WE HOPE THAT THIS BOOK OFFERS SOME OPTIMISM ABOUT THE FUTURE OF SCHOOLING AND THE WAYS IN WHICH EDUCATORS CAN IMPACT THE LIVES OF THEIR STUDENTS.

It's too trite to say that time will heal all wounds. These wounds are part of us now, but they don't have to define our future.

In order to rebound, we need to address the collective experiences we have had, including those that were traumatic, and rebuild our sense of self. We need to help our students do the same. And we need to recover and reassemble our students' learning. We can choose to see this as an opportunity to positively change schooling and learning for more students. To do so, we need to take what we have learned and create a new language of schooling. Let's not simply go back to school but rather return to school stronger and better. Our schools are on the rebound.

Yes, we hope that this book offers some optimism about the future of schooling and the ways in which educators can impact the lives of their students. And we hope that this book helps you recognize the wounds, address them as well as you can, and take what we have collectively learned to improve the overall quality of schooling.

THE "NEXT NORMAL"

Over the past several decades, there have been instances in which members of society have argued that there will be a "new normal." There is much debate about who first developed the phrase, but it has been used following the 2001 World Trade Center bombings, the 2005 avian influenza, the 2008 financial crisis, and many others. McNamee suggests that "the new normal is a time of substantial possibilities if you are willing to play by the new roles for the long term" (Sartain, 2004, p. 1). But the current twin pandemics of disease and the recognition of systematic racism (Williams & Youmans, 2020), as well as the imminent restricting of the global economic order (Sneader & Singhal, 2020), require that we consider the "next normal," which is meant to reframe our thinking from getting "back to business" to imagining what the next normal will be like. Those writing about the next normal, mostly in business, describe an arch with several stages (see Figure 1). These stages apply to the work we're doing here and now and include the following:

- **Resolve.** At this first stage, we recognize what is. This includes acknowledgment of what has been lost and what the world looks like now. We give ourselves permission to mourn the things that are gone, yet we make a decision to move forward. As we will see in the first module, this includes recovering from the traumas we have experienced and accepting the facts, including the need to improve the learning lives of our students.

- **Relief and resilience.** As we move into this second stage, we experience some relief and mobilize our resilience. We begin to recognize that we can face challenges and that we rely on our personal, professional, and collective assets to protect ourselves from the effects of the stressors that continue to exist. As we have noted before, the impact of these world events will leave a mark and, with support and connection with others, we can use what we learned to improve schooling.

- **Return and reopen.** As we begin planning for and implementing the reopening of schools and return more and more students to physical classrooms, we experience a range of emotions—nostalgia, loss, joy, and more. We're thrilled to see our students repopulate the campus yet recognize that learning environments have changed. Some students did much better with distance learning, academically and socially, and may choose to continue online. Others craved the social interactions of school or needed more support from a teacher. Still others need significant social and emotional support to re-engage with learning. As we reopen, we realize that distance, hybrid, hyflex, remote, blended, and simultaneous learning will continue to be options for some, or many, students. This realization, that school will never be the same as we knew it in the before times, can test our resilience and passion. But, if we embrace the possibilities, we can move forward to reimagining our classrooms.

- **Reimagine.** As we come to terms with the next normal, we start reimagining the ways in which learning can occur. We think about students' ownership of their learning and their ability to self-regulate as they choose strategies for learning, seek feedback, and monitor their progress. We look at what worked for our students in distance learning and what didn't. If we let ourselves, we can get excited about what the future holds and the ways in which these crises can open the doors of possibility for students. We embrace the lessons learned from pandemics and engage students in lessons that build their skills, identity, intellectualism, criticality, and joy (Muhammad, 2020).

- **Redefine and reinvent.** As we embrace the possibilities that we imagine, we begin to redefine school and reinvent ourselves, our classrooms, the learning experiences students have, the ways schools operate, and the very idea of schooling itself. We are emboldened, and we take action. We recognize the harm that has been done and create new opportunities for ourselves and our students. And hopefully, we never go back to the way that schooling was. We no longer miss those old days, as our impact has grown and we are realizing success. We recognize effective practices and new approaches, and we implement them.

Figure 1 The Next Normal for Schooling

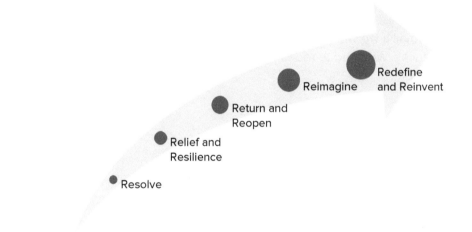

WHY THIS BOOK?

This is a playbook, meaning that it is designed for you to interact with. There are tasks, reflection opportunities, and tools that you can use to move forward, personally and professionally, in the ways that we described above.

In the first module, we focus on the ways in which we heal from trauma. From there, we move to agency—the belief that your actions result in good things.

Both educators and their students' agency have been tested. We ask ourselves, is anything that I'm doing making a difference? Does it matter if I put forth the effort, or will I just fail and fail again? Rebuilding agency is an important part of rebounding schools.

REBUILDING AGENCY IS AN IMPORTANT PART OF REBOUNDING SCHOOLS.

As we rebuild agency, we recognize that we must recover learning for our students and ourselves. As we will note, it remains to be seen how much learning needs to be recovered and by whom. Certainly, some students and educators have suffered greatly. Our current reality is that we need to recover from the lost learning and, in doing so, we need to resist the temptation to focus on gaps, remediation, and lowered expectations. If there ever was a time to believe in the capabilities of our students and ourselves, it is now. We will focus on accelerating learning and creating opportunities for learning leaps.

And finally, in the last module of this playbook, we offer a glimpse of what schools can be. It's time to rethink schooling and use the wisdom collected during this pandemic to make schools even better. We do not subscribe to the idea that schools have been failing all of their students. The majority of students do quite well. But some do not. And, we have to ask, where is the ceiling on learning and have we reached it? We don't believe so. There is much to do, and this should create a sense of excitement.

We cannot unsee what we have seen. The pain, the inequities, the lack of engagement—the list could go on. And this was the case for the old normal and the COVID normal! If we want to survive, and thrive, we need to rebound from these experiences. We need to redefine and reinvent. The time is now. The opportunity is ours.

MODULE 1

REBOUND

Traumatic events can take a heavy toll on our psychological lives. We recognize and respond to the one-time events that devastate our lives: a fire, an injury, the death of a loved one, a violent attack. But less recognizable, even to oneself, is the cost of relentless stress. The pandemic has created chronic, long-term stress in our personal and professional lives. This can lead to a variety of health problems (American Psychological Association, 2018).

It began with the heroic responses of educators all over the world in March 2020. In a matter of weeks, schooling shifted to the crisis teaching that marked the spring. Remember when we all thought that it would last about three weeks and then we'd be able to return to school? As the pandemic deepened, schools had to face the reality that some version of virtual learning would continue well into 2021. Our learning curve was steep. We gained new digital competencies, figured out what it meant to work from home, and in many cases absorbed the added stressor of being a parent of our own children in distance learning. We put one foot in front of the other, driven by a sense of responsibility for the learning lives of young people.

We're here to say something shocking: *It's not all about the kids.* Your emotional and physical well-being is foundational to everything else. With all the pressures we face as a field about our students and schools (disrupted learning, inequitable schooling, the impact on vulnerable students and communities), rebounding begins with taking care of *you*.

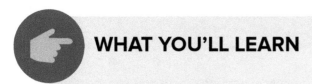

WHAT YOU'LL LEARN

LEARNING INTENTIONS

- I am learning about the psychological and emotional costs that ongoing stress and complex trauma create.

- I am learning about optimal levels of autonomy in teaching.

- I am learning about three avenues of healthy response to stress and trauma.

- I am learning how to support others who are struggling.

SUCCESS CRITERIA

- I can identify actions for maintaining and healing my psychological self.

- I can talk with others who may be struggling.

SELF-ASSESSMENT

Use the provided scale to identify your level of knowledge about complex trauma. Consider each of these statements:

- I am aware of the physical and psychological costs of ongoing stress and complex trauma.

- I know about the role of autonomy in the professional lives of educators.

- I have strategies for holding a conversation with a person who is emotionally struggling.

NEW TERRITORY

There are some industries that regularly experience rapid and unexpected changes, often marked by disasters. For example, aviation, energy, and military organizations are structured in part to absorb and respond to crises and sudden reversals in their work. Leaders in those industries will tell you that the goal in a disaster is not to seek control but rather order. Education is not one of those fields. In fact, we pride ourselves on the steadiness of our field and its role in society. The pandemic changed all that.

We found ourselves as a field in new territory with no guidebook to turn to. Schooling as we know it sustained a seismic shift that profoundly altered the way we taught, collaborated, solved problems, and measured our performance. As we return to a growing degree of face-to-face learning, we are still operating in uncharted waters.

In some ways, we may be our own worst enemies when it comes to managing our own recovery. There is shockingly little research on the role of trauma in the lives of teachers. Mind you, there is lots of work on trauma *and* teachers. There has been much attention, and rightly so, on the importance of trauma-sensitive teaching practices. And there is a growing body of research on secondary traumatic stress and compassion fatigue among educators who work with traumatized students (Essary et al., 2020). But as an industry we have experienced relatively little of the kinds of complex traumas associated with other professions, such as health care and first responders. Therefore, we have relatively little in the way of infrastructure or policies that address our own traumas head on (see Wiliam, 2020). Not our students' trauma—our own.

The education profession values, if not overtly, the image of the altruistic teacher who puts their own well-being aside in order to focus exclusively on students. Think of the movies you've seen. From *Goodbye, Mr. Chips* to *Stand and Deliver* to *The Miracle Worker*, a heroic and utterly selfless teacher makes an enormous difference in the life of a student. Rarely do we see stories about teachers who monitor their own well-being in healthy ways. Instead, the story goes, any healing is derived solely from the act of teaching. That is a narrative that must be discarded. We must acknowledge the traumas we have suffered in order to take healthy steps to rebound.

THE COST OF COMPLEX TRAUMA

As educators, we have worked under highly stressful conditions for more than a year. This can result in a complex trauma that is the result of ongoing stressors. The evidence on the effects of chronic stress points to physical consequences, including cardiovascular disease, disrupted sleep, skin

problems, and fatigue. The effects on mental health are significant, too, and are marked by mood disorders, heightened anxiety, relationship problems, difficulty in concentration, and disconnecting from others. It is likely that the overload, the mounting stressors, the lack of attention to how teachers and school leaders have coped during COVID teaching, and the extra demands of any rebound and return to the classroom can trigger more leaving the profession. This is the time to attend to the manner of coping, the recognition, time, and resources needed to attend to these issues.

The research on stress has long turned from the stressors (pandemic teaching, the competing demands of teaching and parenting in the same rooms, etc.) to the coping strategies reacting to the stressors. This is why some teachers with the same stress conditions can have markedly different reactions.

Please keep in mind that your responses to the chronic stress and complex trauma that you have experienced are normal responses to an abnormal situation. The very good news is that most people do recover from trauma with help. This help includes marshaling internal and external resources. People who are not able to recover from a complex trauma can experience more long-term consequences, notably posttraumatic stress disorder (PTSD).

YOUR RESPONSES TO THE CHRONIC STRESS AND COMPLEX TRAUMA THAT YOU HAVE EXPERIENCED ARE NORMAL RESPONSES TO AN ABNORMAL SITUATION.

PAUSE & PONDER

How Are You Managing?

Please take a few minutes to gauge your responses during this last year. Have any of these symptoms occurred since COVID teaching started?

PHYSICAL RESPONSES	YES	NO	PSYCHOLOGICAL RESPONSES	YES	NO
I have difficulty sleeping.	X		My emotional responses are more intense.		X
My healthy eating habits have declined.		X	I have trouble concentrating.		X
I consume more alcohol or drugs.		X	My closest personal relationships have suffered.		X
I exercise less frequently.		X	I experience anxiety more frequently.		X

BURNOUT AND AUTONOMY

Unrelenting stress manifests itself in our teaching lives, too. It can lead to professional burnout, which is in response to not coping with the stressors experienced on the job, including workload and working conditions, feelings of isolation, and lack of support or recognition. These stressors have a snowball effect. It may begin with emotional exhaustion, which in turn can foster cynical beliefs. These negative attitudes can provoke a desire to withdraw contact, leading to a lower sense of efficacy (Bermejo-Toro et al., 2016). You may have experienced some of these conditions previously (workload, etc.), but they didn't lead to emotional exhaustion and burnout. So why now? The answer, in a word, is a loss—a loss of sense of control or sense of worthwhileness. An important antidote to burnout is a sense of predictability over our choices of actions and priorities, which serves as a counterbalance (Simões & Calheiros, 2019). Take a few minutes to consider where you have been and where you are now using six measures of perceived autonomy adapted from the US Department of Education on its Schools and Staffing Survey.

PAUSE & PONDER

Use the traffic light scale to reflect on your perceived autonomy before and during the pandemic.

BEFORE THE PANDEMIC	How much actual control do you have **in your classroom** at this school over the following areas of your planning and teaching?	DURING THE PANDEMIC
	Selecting instructional materials and their use	
	Selecting content, topics, and skills to be taught	
	Selecting teaching techniques	
	Evaluating and grading students	

BEFORE THE PANDEMIC	How much actual control do you have **in your classroom** at this school over the following areas of your planning and teaching?	DURING THE PANDEMIC
———————/—	Establishing classroom procedures and addressing problematic behavior	———————/—
———————/—	Determining the amount of classwork and practice to be assigned	———————/—

Of course, complete autonomy is not a good thing. Schoolwide policies and standards govern much of what it is that we do as educators and serve as guardrails that guide the work. Consistency across some aspects of schooling can help students learn. A school that fosters an "anything goes" approach is not going to get breakthrough results. In fact, it undermines what we know about collective teacher efficacy, which is the knowledge a team has that they possess the wherewithal to effect positive change. However, low levels of autonomy are also problematic and contribute to feelings of loss of efficacy and to a professional paralysis. You may have noticed in your reflection that you experienced and may still be experiencing some loss of autonomy during COVID teaching. Or perhaps you gained autonomy. You may be feeling that you had more opportunities to try out innovative practices. It's not just the lack of, or increase in, autonomy but rather how we cope with the experiences. With strong coping strategies, these are less a source of stress.

LOW LEVELS OF AUTONOMY ARE PROBLEMATIC AND CONTRIBUTE TO FEELINGS OF LOSS OF EFFICACY AND TO A PROFESSIONAL PARALYSIS.

CASE IN POINT

The teaching staff at Ridgefield Junior High have experienced a full school year of distance COVID teaching. Since the school first closed in March 2020, every student has been a virtual learner. The building itself was closed periodically throughout the year, meaning that teachers taught from home. Because it was optional where teachers reported from, some taught solely from home, while others taught from their empty classrooms. The return to face-to-face instruction has meant that colleagues are reconnecting and reacquainting themselves with one another. A handful of staff were hired during the pandemic, and this marks the first time they have seen others in person.

One ongoing conversation has been in identifying successful processes and practices that emerged during distance learning. There was widespread agreement that schoolwide practices for student collaboration were an important innovation (Fisher et al., 2020a, 2020b). During the first weeks of school closure, the instructional leadership team (ILT), which consisted of grade-level representatives, the instructional coach, and an administrator, identified student collaboration practices that could be taught and utilized across content areas. The team called these "spotlight practices" because they believed these would be high-utility routines across content areas. These methods do not require students to be physically present, aim to develop their independence as well as collective efficacy skills, and can be optimized using social media platforms. The instructional methods promoted and used included *teach-back*, *text rendering*, *fishbowl discussions*, *jigsaw*, and *5-word summaries*. Their professional learning meetings through the spring focused on teaching staff these strategies for use in their virtual classrooms.

James Lincoln, a seventh-grade science teacher, expressed a sentiment held by many: "It really helped that the other teachers I shared students with were also using these strategies." This allowed teachers over time to spend less time on *instructions* for collaborative tasks and more time for *instruction*. "My kids seemed to get the hang of these in a matter of weeks. And they learned how to do this online, so I'm going to keep using these strategies in class and virtually. They love the opportunity to teach-back to their family or the class, for example."

But Trish Carson, an eighth-grade math teacher, spoke for others when she said, "Not all the strategies were useful for me. I really didn't use text rendering [a process for clarifying text], but I felt I had to because others were doing it. I want to be a team player, but that one wasn't practical." Robin McCafferty, a member of the ILT and a ninth-grade English teacher, suggested that they co-construct a new list of spotlight practices. Staff members nominated other instructional strategies for consideration.

REFLECT

How would you advise the staff at Ridgefield to proceed? Keep in mind what you know about the role of autonomy in teaching.

Similar to students, teachers need voice & choice in their instructional practice.

RECOVERING FROM COMPLEX TRAUMA

Van der Kolk (2015) notes in his book, *The Body Keeps the Score*, that there are three possible healthy avenues a person might take in response to stress and trauma (p. 3):

1. **Top-down,** by talking, (re-)connecting with others, and allowing ourselves to know and understand what is going on with us.

2. By taking **medicines** that shut down inappropriate alarm reactions, or by utilizing other technologies that change the way the brain organizes information.

3. **Bottom-up,** by allowing the body to have experiences that deeply and viscerally contradict the helplessness, rage, or collapse that result from trauma.

To these three, we add becoming aware of the coping strategies that have been, are, and could be used. When the focus of our stressor changes, our time-honored ways of coping are often no longer appropriate. Working with others to be aware of these strategies, trying new ones, and incorporating a range of coping strategies is an important factor in recovering.

Our colleague Sandi Everlove talks about the importance of daily acts of hope, renewal, and discovery in taking steps forward to rebound. Van der Kolk's first and third avenues track closely with Everlove's advice. The second avenue is also important. Additional professional therapeutic supports can be a vital conduit for recovery. We are not mental health experts. In the rest of this module, we will discuss ways in which you can address your experiences. But please keep in mind these questions offered by the American Psychological Association (2017) for consideration in pursuing therapy from a licensed professional. They note that two factors should be taken into account: (1) Is the problem distressing? (2) Is it interfering with some aspect of your life?

When thinking about distress, here are some issues to consider:
• Do you or someone close to you spend some amount of time every week thinking about the problem?
• Is the problem embarrassing, to the point that you want to hide from others?
• Over the past few months, has the problem reduced your quality of life?

When thinking about interference, some other issues may deserve consideration:
• Does the problem take up considerable time (e.g., more than an hour per day)?
• Have you curtailed your work or educational ambitions because of the problem?
• Are you rearranging your lifestyle to accommodate the problem?

Bottling up our feelings, not sharing any sense of building pressure, and imagining we can resolve everything ourselves is not healthy. Yes, we may be "very competent" teachers, know that we are great at dealing with the pressures and demands once the classroom door is closed; but COVID teaching is different, may require different ways of thinking, and we may need to share our thinking, problems, and collectively develop new strategies.

In the 1980s, when students with disabilities were moved from "special classes" to mainstream classes (such old language), the teachers who suffered burnout and left the profession were those who could not talk to their colleagues about how to work with these students, how to incorporate them into regular classes and not reduce quality for the other students (Forlin et al., 1996). COVID teaching is different, and sometimes different solutions are needed.

RECOVERY FROM COMPLEX TRAUMA: TOP-DOWN APPROACHES

One avenue of recovery is what van der Kolk (2015) calls top-down approaches. These are ways in which people promote their own socialization efforts. Being around other people, especially those who care for and about you, is one of the very best ways to engage in the kind of self-care necessary for healing.

ISOLATING ONESELF FROM OTHERS CAN HASTEN A DOWNWARD SPIRAL.

Keep isolation at bay. It can be tempting to withdraw from contact with other people and situations in order to reduce the feelings caused by relentless stress and complex trauma. To be sure, having some self-soothing techniques can assist you in moving through a difficult moment (it's okay once in a while to pull the covers up over your head). But isolating oneself from others can hasten a downward spiral. Being with other people doesn't mean that you have to talk about what is causing you distress. Your participation in social events is good for others, and it is good for you. Reach out to old friends or former colleagues that you haven't been in touch with lately to reconnect. If there is one thing we have all learned during the months of isolation, it is that outreach efforts are welcome. As we move into the next stages of recovery, keep up those emotional muscles you've been developing to maintain these practices.

Volunteer in your community. One of the hallmarks of educators in general is a service mindset. None of us got into the field with the idea that it would be the path to monetary wealth (although we also did not take a vow of poverty). What has drawn so many to the profession is that it fulfills a need to serve others and to make the world a better place. That same spirit of generosity draws many educators and other service-oriented individuals to volunteer their time and talents. Studies on volunteerism note that those who do so possess a higher degree of generativity (being productive), a psychological sense of community (being connected), and empathy (Omoto & Packard, 2016).

Check in regularly on your own emotions. The return to school is something we have all longed for, but the return is also likely to spark some unexpected negative feelings. You may experience a heightened level of anxiety about being in closer proximity to so many people after such a long period of physical distancing. As well, the euphoria you had anticipated for so long may not materialize. Be sure to check in on your own emotions more frequently during this transition time. Your resilience is being stretched a bit thinner than usual. And remember to check in on your colleagues as they might need a little extra help now and then.

RECOVERY FROM COMPLEX TRAUMA: BOTTOM-UP APPROACHES

A second avenue for psychological healing is to bring the physical body into the game. The mind–body connection is well-known even within the popular culture, and it makes good sense that examining physical health habits can improve mental health. Words like "heartbreak" and "gut-wrenching" are in our language for a reason—they speak to our subconscious understanding that mind and body are linked (van der Kolk, 2015).

Make sure you move every day. Some people established new exercise routines during the pandemic to make sure they were mindful of movement. If so, keep your routine going as you return to school! If you didn't, find ways to incorporate thirty minutes of exercise each day. It doesn't have to be the same routine. It can be a combination of walking, cycling, working with weights, or dancing at home to your favorite tunes. The rhythmic element of activities like these is good for you physically and, at the same time, can clear your mind. Keep in mind that a return to classroom teaching requires a bit more stamina than you may currently have.

A RETURN TO CLASSROOM TEACHING REQUIRES A BIT MORE STAMINA THAN YOU MAY CURRENTLY HAVE.

Recalibrate your sleep routines. Returning to face-to-face instruction requires some adjustments to your morning and evening routines. You may have to get up earlier to accommodate the commute, which is longer than the walk to the home workspace you used for so long. Your evening routine is probably undergoing a change as well. It's easy to sacrifice sleep in order to get everything done. Use the following chart from the Sleep Foundation as a guide to how much sleep you and the people in your household should be getting.

Age	Recommended	May be appropriate	Not recommended
Newborns *0–3 months*	14 to 17 hours	11 to 13 hours 18 to 19 hours	Less than 11 hours More than 19 hours
Infants *4–11 months*	12 to 15 hours	10 to 11 hours 16 to 18 hours	Less than 10 hours More than 18 hours
Toddlers *1–2 years*	11 to 14 hours	9 to 10 hours 15 to 16 hours	Less than 9 hours More than 16 hours
Preschoolers *3–5 years*	10 to 13 hours	8 to 9 hours 14 hours	Less than 8 hours More than 14 hours
School-Age Children *6–13 years*	9 to 11 hours	7 to 8 hours 12 hours	Less than 7 hours More than 12 hours
Teenagers *14–17 years*	8 to 10 hours	7 hours 11 hours	Less than 7 hours More than 11 hours
Young Adults *18–25 years*	7 to 9 hours	6 hours 10 to 11 hours	Less than 6 hours More than 11 hours
Adults *26–64 years*	7 to 9 hours	6 hours 10 hours	Less than 6 hours More than 10 hours
Older Adults *≥65 years*	7 to 8 hours	5 to 6 hours 9 hours	Less than 5 hours More than 9 hours

Source: Adapted from Sleep Foundation (www.sleepfoundation.org).

Make healthy eating part of your routine. Food habits can suffer as schedules change, as quick and convenient may outpace the need to make conscious food and eating decisions. They are even more likely to suffer in the face of ongoing stress. The emerging field of nutritional psychiatry specializes in the relationship between the quality of a person's diet and their risk for depression and other common mental disorders, specifically the "microbiome-gut-brain axis" (Jacka, 2017, p. 24). Attend to the food you eat and the way it makes you feel to gain a better sense of the foods that may trigger fatigue, sluggishness, or a reduced ability to concentrate.

 CASE IN POINT

The science department at Barton High School consists of seven educators who have taught together for the past decade. They have been present at each other's family celebrations and attended funerals when one of their members has lost a parent. When their school had to close because of the pandemic, they found themselves isolated from one another for the first time. "I was so used to seeing them every morning," said chemistry teacher Ray Linnea. "I never really appreciated how important these people were to me."

The team found their way back to each other during the months of working from home, in part because the leadership provided space and time for them to do so. They established a weekly virtual coffee break for anyone to drop in and set up occasional watch parties featuring movies to view together. Earth science teacher Tim Foster said, "There were some weeks where this was a major highlight for me. Something to look forward to."

Another earth science teacher, Kendra Prince, knew that some of her colleagues were runners. She did some research and located a virtual race club that had the kind of flexibility that would make it possible for a range of fitness levels. Two other members of the department joined her on these virtual runs throughout the summer. "It gave us another point of contact and conversation," she said. Biology teacher Teresa Ruiz made a vegetable gardening challenge to other members. "We had lots of jokes about our '$600 tomatoes,' but it sparked some really good creativity. One of my colleagues lives in a small apartment, and she got really inventive about gardening in pots on her balcony," she said. "It also fulfilled a mission we all have for our students—to connect with the natural world."

REFLECT

Now the Barton High science team has returned to face-to-face instruction. What are some of the strategies they used to stay socially connected and physically healthy? What advice would you give to them about the importance of maintaining these habits during this time of transition?

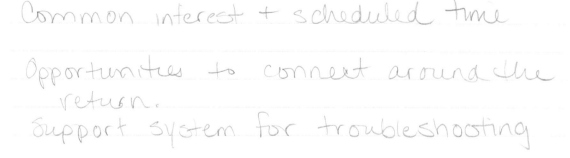

Common interest + scheduled time

Opportunities to connect around the return.

Support system for troubleshooting

SHOWING SUPPORT TO OTHERS

The challenges our colleagues are facing weigh on each of us, too. However, it can feel awkward to talk with them about their well-being. Many of us hold some rigid notions of professional lives versus personal ones and are reluctant to cross an unstated boundary. Our own experience with teaching and writing about adult social and emotional learning (SEL) is that most educators want to turn the discussion back to their students rather than sit with their own feelings. This is a characteristic of our profession—we keep a steady lens on students. But if we don't expand our focus to include colleagues, we condemn people to wrestle with personal challenges in isolation.

We don't expect you to suddenly become a therapist, or worse yet, to start diagnosing others. But your willingness to open a line of communication with a colleague who you believe is struggling may very well be a light for them. Don't be afraid that you might not say the exact right thing. Your demonstration of caring sends a powerful message to them. Having a few statements or questions in mind can open up the conversation. Remember, it is the power of listening that matters more than talking about the solutions. A fundamental aspect of respect and dignity is the ability to listen and communicate that you have listened. (It is no different for many students who want you to listen to them—listen to how they are solving problems and not have you rush in with the right answer—they know there is a right answer; it is their thinking that is not leading to the right answer that is their concern—and listening to how they are thinking and processing is what they want you to do to then help them work to the right answers).

Elmer (2019) advises that these can be especially helpful in guiding your conversation:

- **Do you want to talk about it? I'm here when you're ready.** This is more direct than simply asking, "Are you okay?" which can tempt the stock reply, "I'm fine."

- **What can I do to help today?** Sometimes doing a simple task together, such as giving a hand at organizing your colleague's class library, can serve as a way to establish a safe space for conversation.

- **How are you managing?** This question allows you to acknowledge a person's struggles without having to list them.

- **You're not alone. I may not understand exactly how you feel, but you're not alone.** This counters the temptation to turn the spotlight on yourself and your own challenges. When you're reaching out to someone who you suspect needs support, don't try to match their challenges with your own.

- **That sounds like it's really hard. How are you coping?** Your colleague may name something in particular that they are having difficulty working through. Don't tell them what you did in a similar circumstance; just listen.

- **I'm really sorry you're going through this. I'm here for you if you need me.** Keep the line of communication open. It isn't realistic to believe that a single conversation is going to resolve everything for the person. Complex traumas can't be resolved that way. Letting that person know that you are part of their caring network matters.

CASE IN POINT

Layla Rasheed is returning to face-to-face instruction with her fifth-grade students. It has been a difficult year for the community. Many of the families at her school are essential workers, and the pandemic has been especially devastating. Children have lost family members, and others have suffered from housing and food insecurities. Ms. Rasheed's personal experiences during the pandemic have been trying. She lost four family members in the past year and has been coordinating efforts to support her elderly grandmother, including running errands, shopping for food, and transporting the woman to medical appointments in order to minimize time spent in public spaces.

The teacher's professional life has been a monumental challenge as well. The first months of school closures were focused on getting devices and connectivity to vulnerable students. Ms. Rasheed served on a district committee to create a supply chain for students. In the fall, the school reopened for face-to-face instruction but had to shift to distance learning less than a month into the school year when cases surged. In the months since, Ms. Rasheed and her students shifted to a hybrid schedule to minimize the number of students in the building. In addition, she did simultaneous teaching with students who participated virtually. Her three children are also students in the district and experienced similar disruptions throughout the year.

INSIDE EVERY CRISIS IS AN OPPORTUNITY.

As she returns to a new school year, she is already exhausted, even though instruction has not yet begun. The normally celebratory first staff meetings have been muted. One staff member died last year, and several others chose not to return to teaching at all. She is reminded of these losses each time she looks around the room. In addition, health protocols are still in place, so the extra cleaning, physical distancing, and mask wearing are constant reminders that the return to school is not a return to the way school looked pre-pandemic.

Imagine you are a trusted colleague of Ms. Rasheed's, and you have sensed that all is not well with her. She has told you that she isn't feeling recharged like she normally does at the start of a new school year. You know about the personal challenges she has faced, too. As a caring colleague and friend, you want to have a conversation with her about her well-being.

REFLECT

How will you prepare for the conversation? What do you want to be sure to do and say? What do you want to be sure not to do or say?

SAY/DO	DON'T SAY/DON'T DO
offer to listen acknowledge challenge	compare my experience

SPRING FORWARD

Inside every crisis is an opportunity. One opportunity we have is to re-engage with our emotional lives to strengthen our resiliency and recover from relentless stress and complex traumas. We have been through much, personally and professionally. Our efforts to rebound and strengthen schooling begin with an investment in ourselves. Before leaving this module, reflect on your learning about your relationship with *you*.

REFLECT

Reflect on your learning in this module. Identify actions you are considering based on your learning.

IMPORTANT

On a scale of 1 to 5, with 5 being very important and 1 being not important at all, how would you rate the value of addressing the emotional and psychological needs of yourself and other adults in your school?

1   2   3   4   5

WAIT, BUT WHY?

Explain your reason for the rating above.

MODULE 2

REBUILDING EDUCATOR AGENCY

We all want to experience success in our professional lives. When we exert energy and effort, we expect good things to happen. If we plan lessons, identify powerful instructional strategies, and engage our students, we expect that they will learn. And when we see evidence of that learning, we make the connection between our efforts and the impact that these efforts have.

When we don't experience the link between our efforts and the impact that they have, our efficacy and agency are reduced. Over time, we come to believe that our efforts are not the deciding factor in students' learning, and we might even think that our efforts are pointless.

When that happens, we start to burn out. Burnout is not the result of how many hours that you work. It's more related to the effort and impact connection. When we work hard and see outcomes, our efficacy and agency grow. And the reverse is also true. When we don't see outcomes we value from the efforts we put forth, our efficacy and agency are reduced. When this continues, we become demoralized and perhaps even leave the profession.

A few definitions are in order. **Efficacy** is "a person's sense of being able to deal effectively with a particular task" (Woolfolk, 2007, p. 332). **Agency** is the ability to engage in efforts to reach a goal, which can include impacting others. Both are important, but efficacy does not seem to be as significantly compromised as agency as a result of the pandemics. We need to re-establish the link between teacher actions and student learning.

WHAT YOU'LL LEARN

LEARNING INTENTIONS

- I am learning about efficacy and how to build it.
- I am learning about rebuilding agency via collaboration, feedback, and a focus on success.

SUCCESS CRITERIA

- I can analyze the sources of efficacy and plan to improve my own efficacy.
- I can develop collaborative structures and interact with colleagues.
- I can seek and provide feedback.
- I can harvest wins and attribute success to the efforts.

SELF-ASSESSMENT

Using the provided scale, identify your level of knowledge about educator agency. Consider each of these statements:

- I am aware of the influencers on efficacy.

- I understand agency and power of agency in my practice.

- I understand the impact of collaboration with colleagues on agency.

- I understand the impact of feedback on agency.

- I understand the impact of linking effort with success on agency.

EFFICACY

According to hundreds of thousands of studies summarized in the Visible Learning® research, teachers have the greatest impact on learning within schools. In other words, you matter. And the decisions you make and the actions you take can accelerate students' learning. And principals, you matter too, as you have the potential to magnify and multiply effective teaching (Manna, 2015). Let's not forget that. We'll start with efficacy or your confidence that you can have an impact on all students. Bandura (1982) identified four sources of efficacy:

1. **Mastery experiences.** This is the most powerful source in building efficacy. It's the direct experiences we have that show that we can successfully complete a task. For example, when you work through your thinking and figure out the success criteria necessary for students to understand how they will know that they've learned something, and then your students achieve these criteria, you experience a sense of mastery, and it contributes to your efficacy.

2. **Vicarious experiences or modeling.** When you see someone else accomplish something, and you realize that you can do something very similar, you build a sense of efficacy. This is further enhanced when the person modeling possesses similar characteristics or skills as you. For example, when your colleague shares a video clip of her modeling, you hear her thinking and decision making, and you see students applying the strategies, you might say to yourself, "I can do that," and then give it a try.

3. **Social persuasion.** This occurs when others give you a pep talk of sorts. It's the encouragement that you receive from others that shapes your belief that you can accomplish a task: for example, when your grade-level team examines student writing samples and agrees that students need to learn more about various ways to introduce their topic and someone shares a list of introduction types. Another person says, "We can do this. I didn't know that there were so many ways. This will be much easier to teach with this information." And you say to yourself, "That's right; it will be," and your efficacy increases.

4. **Physiological factors.** Sometimes there is a feeling of excitement and the sense that you are ready for the task ahead. This increases efficacy, whereas a sense of anxiety and foreboding decreases efficacy. For many of us, the fear of technology and the comparison of our virtual learning classes with others (especially that amazing teacher on social media who always seemed to have it going on) has decreased our efficacy because of

the physiological response. As an alternative, when you experience some excitement that the task will be rewarding and that students will engage with the learning, your efficacy grows. People with a higher degree of self-efficacy are better equipped to manage these physiological factors. Remember the butterflies you had when you used a virtual breakout room with your students? As you grew more comfortable, those butterflies became more manageable.

What have you noticed about your own sense of self-efficacy? What experiences have you had that have contributed to your sense of self-efficacy? What experiences have lowered it?

Experiences That Build My Self-Efficacy	Experiences That Lower My Self-Efficacy
•	•
•	•
•	•

CASE IN POINT

Sixth-grade teacher Thomas Chavez was excited about the unit he was designing. It focused on resistance and liberation through knowledge, and one of the lessons focused on the question: *What is knowledge, and what can we accept as evidence?* He wanted his students to understand fake news and the ways in which discoveries are validated. Another lesson focused on building a global knowledge base. Students would be introduced to the House of Wisdom in Baghdad and the work of early Muslim scholars. As Mr. Chavez said, "I was in a training, and one of the breakout room conversations really got me going. Another teacher shared her plans and her thinking about her teaching about fake news, and it really got me thinking. That's a really important lesson for my students as well. She shared her whole plan and her notes about her thinking and what she was looking for via Google Docs, and I was able to build off that. Actually, I think that this is going to be better than what I had planned before. I couldn't even sleep that night after the training as I was excited to try this new lesson." Note the vicarious experience Mr. Chavez had. And note the physiological aspect of his excitement.

When he shared ideas with his team, one of his colleagues said, "I've been wondering how to better present the history of science, especially the early Muslim scholars. I really like the idea of a global knowledge base so that students don't think Europeans thought up everything. Ideas were being developed around the world at about the same time, and I think it would be great to trace the ways that knowledge is created and shared." This social persuasion was highly reinforcing for Mr. Chavez.

But the mastery experience came when students started talking with their families about fake news and how to decide if the information was accurate. As Mr. Chavez said, "I got some pushback from families. They wanted to be sure that I was not pushing an agenda. When we talked about the need to understand credible sources and the use of evidence in their arguments, they all agreed that it was worthwhile learning. And it felt great. A unit that I developed, inspired by a person I only met virtually, made me feel really good about my efforts." And there is the mastery experience.

Increased efficacy does not require all four of these components to be in play at all times. They each contribute to a sense of efficacy. The idea is to notice them and recognize when efficacy is being built and when it's not.

REFLECT

What experiences have you had that built your efficacy? Develop some ideas for strengthening your efficacy based on the interactions you have with students and with colleagues.

Ways I can strengthen my self-efficacy in my interactions with students this school year:

Ways I can strengthen my self-efficacy in my interactions with colleagues this school year:

As we have noted, efficacy is important, but our sense of agency is even more so. We must re-establish the link between effort and impact. There are three ways to do so. We need to rebuild our collaboration with colleagues, receive and respond to feedback, and recognize our success.

COLLABORATION

Well-meaning leaders in many school systems reduced the expectations that teachers collaborate in recognition of the stress teachers were under and the need to devote time to designing learning experiences for students. The unintended consequence of this has been a reduction in teacher collaboration as grade levels and departments, professional learning communities, and professional learning time. As a result, teacher agency suffered because teachers and leaders needed time to tell their stories and to discuss practices but had no outlet to do so. Agency does not mean "doing it yourself" or creating time to "work it out yourself." Agency means having others listening to your thinking, the problems you are working on, and attributing success or otherwise to your actions and thinking. (As a profession, we are sometimes not good at attributing success to teacher thinking. We credit the students, the parents, the resources, but so much is a response to successful teaching—school leaders have a critical role in giving credit to excellent teaching.)

Without this time to share stories and discuss practice, teachers felt and still may continue to feel isolated. They were not sure if others were experiencing the same challenges and successes that they were. And when groups did meet, there was a tendency to tell horror stories and even one-up each other about how bad things were. We are not dismissing the realities that some students and educators faced, but the lack of collaboration around practice and the impact of those practices damaged teachers' sense of agency, resulting in teachers asking themselves and their leaders, "Are my efforts resulting in anything that matters?"

Of course, there are exceptions, and these exceptions highlight the protective power of collaboration. When teams of teachers were provided time to interact with peers and had systems for telling stories that balanced success and challenge, their agency survived and, in some cases, even thrived. Regardless of the situation that you were in or still may be in, it's time to rebuild collaborative experiences with colleagues as one way to rebuild agency.

We have argued that there are questions that drive the collaborative conversations that teachers have, including (Fisher et al., 2020a):

1. Where are we going?

2. Where are we now?

3. How do we move learning forward?

4. What did we learn today?

5. Who benefited and who did not benefit?

These questions provide space for educators to tell their stories and practices. And they ensure that the conversations move to impact. Here's some additional information about these questions and how they foster collaboration (Fisher et al., 2020b, pp. 8–9).

1. **Where are we going?** This first question is critical. Teams that can answer this question have high levels of teacher clarity. They are keenly aware of the academic standards their students are held accountable to, and they have analyzed these standards to ensure a thorough understanding of the skills, concepts, and rigor levels that lie within each standard. That clarity is used to drive the engineering of learning tasks so that evidence of student learning can be gathered and used to make instructional inferences moving forward. This work is often guided by pacing guides and supported with a variety of curricular resources. If there is little clarity about the goals (of the session, of any intervention), then there is a far reduced chance of team success.

2. **Where are we now?** In order to answer this question, teams need to have evidence to determine current student proficiency and readiness levels against what they captured in the "Where are we going?" question above. Great diagnosis or discovery of the current situation, recognizing strengths and opportunities, is among the most critical agreements we need to then improve our impact on students. This allows teams to determine appropriate entry points for instruction, starting with where students are and moving them to where they need to be. This may require an inventory of existing assessments to identify current resources your team has access to, as well as determining the assessments that will need to be collaboratively designed by the team members. From there, teams identify a common challenge that will drive inquiry into their students' current learning needs.

IF WE GATHERED AND MET AS A PLC AND DIDN'T LEARN ANYTHING, COULDN'T WE HAVE JUST EMAILED EACH OTHER WHAT WE TALKED ABOUT?

3. **How do we move learning forward?** This question focuses on our teaching practices and the means by which we learn from one another. It directly asks about the magnitude of growth, how much learning, as one of the core messages of the Visible Learning research is that merely improving learning may be trivial. We need to develop ways to know "how much" learning is occurring for each student, which is why concepts of progression, understanding where students are from the outset (diagnosis) to the success criteria, and having debates (particularly with our colleagues) about whether the growth relative to the time invested was sufficient. During the teaching process, learning walks and microteaching are two effective ways to frame the ways in which we analyze our own teaching using the wisdom of peers. However, these are not the only ways to consider how to best move learning forward. We cross-examine the tasks that we have designed for our students by analyzing assignments for rigor and alignment to standards.

4. **What did we learn today?** This is a question often asked of students that has just as much power when asked of the adults. Focusing on this question helps teams to synthesize the information discussed and the data reviewed to examine student progress and achievement. Posing this question to teams helps to ground actions and commitments moving forward. By the same notion, we have to acknowledge the simplicity but significance of this question: *If we gathered and met as a PLC and didn't learn anything, couldn't we have just emailed each other what we talked about?*

5. **Who benefited and who did not benefit?** This question continues the examination of student progress and achievement. At times, students who are already at high levels of achievement are not focused on as much as students who possess large deficits in their learning. Ask yourself, "What strategies and discussions about learning progress did you have with the students above average compared to those below average?" All students need these teaching processes, but of course, they may be quite different discussions. However, growth is something that all students deserve regardless of their current proficiency level. A focus on this question exposes both, thus guiding team members where to go next for each learner. This is an equity question, and addressing it ensures that factors such as race, socioeconomic status, or disability status aren't used as excuses that impede a student's ability to learn. Teams examine the supports designed for students in light of what is working and take action to improve what is not.

CASE IN POINT

A group of high school biology teachers were talking about how to move learning forward, specifically in teaching about cells. Brandi White commented, "We've always had interactive notebooks. It's kinda like a thing here. But we learned a lot about digital notebooks, and I think that the students did really well with them. They were able to complete tasks and take notes no matter where they were. I think we should up our game this year on digital interactive notebooks."

In response, Tessa Jamison said, "I totally agree. I was so impressed with the notes that my students took in their digital notebooks. And their responses on the discussion boards and the quizzes were great. I think we can make them even better this year."

Mike Artilles confessed, "I really didn't use them. I don't know how they work and I'm not sure how to help you all build them."

Ms. Jamison responded, "I can show you how. I don't want to say that they're easy, but once you understand the linking, it works. And we can all share the same notebook. Students just make a copy for themselves and they work on their own version. I can help build them, but I think we need to think about the contents and what we need to provide to really have students learn this content. I am thinking that students can be involved in the development of the notebooks. Do you think that would be a good idea?"

Their conversation continued as teachers shared with one another their experiences and successes. At the end of the meeting, Mr. Artilles added, "It feels like old times to be work with you all like this. I love to hear your thinking about how to use the digital notebooks and how the students responded. But the things we are creating together are better than we've ever done in the past."

REFLECT

How does your team collaborate? What systems do you need to put in place to rebuild collaboration and ensure that teacher agency continues to grow?

FEEDBACK

Learning and growing in a supportive environment also builds agency. We all want to know that we're doing a good job. And we want to know how we can improve to better meet the needs of our students. Unfortunately, during COVID teaching, feedback in many schools and districts was reduced to lessen the stress teachers experienced. And for those who may still be teaching remotely, this may continue to be the case. The unintended consequence of this was that teachers were not sure if they were doing a good job or how to improve. And it's important to recognize that the vast majority of coaches and leaders who could have given feedback had little to no experience in teaching from a distance. But when feedback was provided in an empathetic way, teachers' agency and effectiveness increased.

We're not suggesting that feedback needs to be only from leaders. Peers and coaches can also provide growth-producing feedback that builds teacher agency. And if we work at it, we can provide feedback to ourselves and seek feedback from our students as we reflect on the lessons that we deliver and the impact that those learning experiences have on students. Importantly, one of the best ways to ensure that feedback is received is to ensure that it's based on something that the receiver has asked for. One way we can do this is through a process called microteaching.

Microteaching is the practice of capturing a portion of a lesson or student interaction on video for the purpose of analyzing it. It's a form of feedback from teacher to teacher. A major purpose is to hear aloud the thinking and decision making that occurred during the lesson. The volunteer teacher sets the context of the segment for his colleagues and poses their questions. After viewing, the team asks questions meant to mediate the thinking of the volunteer teacher. The questions should not be thinly veiled evaluations or suggestions but designed to spark the thinking of the volunteer teacher. Many times, this thinking is more focused when watching the video clip with the sound turned off, and this often moves the discussion away from post hoc justification of what the teacher did or thought to deeper discussions. Suggested open-ended questions for the team include (Fisher et al., 2020b, p. 98)

- What did you want your students to know and be able to do?

- What connections have you made?

- What did you see or hear that confirms your previous thinking?

- What did you see or hear that conflicts with your previous thinking?

- Which moments did you find to be particularly effective?

- What was your thinking and decision making at these moments?

- Which moments did you think did not go as well as you had hoped?

- What was different in comparing those moments?

- What would you change in order to accomplish your stated goal?

- What do you want to be sure to do again?

CASE IN POINT

Amanda Hardy is a third-grade teacher. As she says, "The pandemics have been hard on me. I know people who've been sick, and I have argued with my family over social justice issues. I'm not sure that my students were really learning much, even though their scores seemed fine. I decided to show my team members some videos of my teaching to see if there were ways that I could improve. We agreed to focus on vocabulary because our students always seem to need to know more words, and this year is no different. I am okay with focusing on vocabulary, but I didn't think it was that special."

Ms. Hardy selected a five-minute clip from her class in which the students were working with their peers. The students were engaged in a reciprocal teaching experience in which students had specific roles related to comprehension: predicting, summarizing, questioning, and clarifying. This is a common practice in the third grade at her school.

After viewing the clip, one of Ms. Hardy's colleagues asked, "Which moments did you find to be particularly effective?"

Ms. Hardy responded, "Well, I think that their summaries are strong. They seem to understand the text, and that makes me feel good."

Another colleague commented, "You know, their summaries have a lot of key vocabulary. I see them using the words that were the focus of the lesson. Literally, the words are coming out of their mouths, and they are using them in their conversations and in their summaries. Was that part of your goal?"

Ms. Hardy responded, "Not specifically, but I can see that now. Can we watch it again and focus on the vocabulary that the students are using?" The team agreed.

Following their second viewing, a colleague asked, "What do you want to be sure to do again?"

Ms. Hardy responded, "I think that asking them to use the words in their conversations turned out to be important. It wasn't the main message, but I think it worked and I want to be more explicit about it in the future. I'm really glad I picked this clip. It's great to see students' thinking and how they are able to use the vocabulary. I guess it is working. Thank you."

REFLECT

How can you build a great feedback culture on your team? What do you see as the power of feedback for you, whether it is from students, peers, or leaders?

SUCCESS

Success is motivating. When we experience success, we are much more likely to engage in similar tasks, including tasks that are a little harder. That's the whole experience with video games and game apps. The tasks start out a bit easier, and when you've experienced success, they become a little harder. In other words, as you experience success, your agency and use of learning strategies increases, and you are more likely to keep playing that game. Let's take a fictional example. Say there is a game called Dandelion. In this game, you "blow" the seed head, aiming for different targets. At level one, it's pretty easy to hit the target. Once you have experienced success a few times, it gets harder.

If you started at Level 34 on the first try, you would probably be frustrated and not play the game much. But, if weeks later you were still on Level 1, you probably would get bored. The key is to allow people to experience success and then make it harder. The gamers understand increasing agency and the relationship it has to effort.

In our Dandelion example, it's easy for the player to attribute success to their efforts. It's not another person playing the game. I am. I can see the link between my effort and the outcome. In teaching and learning, this link is sometimes harder to see. A key message of Visible Learning is to "know thy impact" in part because understanding the impact that you have reinforces your agency, allows you to make adjustments to increase your impact, and to hold high expectations for yourself and your students.

To rebuild agency, we have to reestablish the link between effort and impact. Doing so requires that we notice and talk about the link. It's easier when others name this for you. But you can do it yourself as well. Consider the following examples of teachers and leaders rebuilding their agency through success:

> TO REBUILD AGENCY, WE HAVE TO REESTABLISH THE LINK BETWEEN EFFORT AND IMPACT.

- When you modeled your thinking, students were able to try on the examples and figure out how to solve the problem.

- When I established routines for collaborative conversations, students took ownership and I did not have to direct their interactions.

- When you provided me feedback, I realized that there were things I was doing well, and it made me feel like a better teacher.

- The students' public speeches were polished and impactful because of the instruction they received from you.

- The information you presented was super organized and I was able to integrate the strategies into my lessons.

Focusing on success and attributing that success to the effort of the individual contributes to the overall agency experienced by the person. That's not to say we ignore areas of growth; those are important as well. But that's what feedback is for. Being a strength-spotter (Linley, 2008), engaging in appreciative inquiry, or harvesting wins, as we like to say, recognizes effort and impact. And, when we make the connection between the two, we can rebuild agency.

CASE IN POINT

Jessica Greene was nominated by her peers as Teacher of the Year for her school. She declined the nomination because she said, "There's nothing good happening in my classroom." Her peers were shocked. Ms. Greene was the most giving person, always sharing lessons and ideas with others. Her students adored her and they always learned a lot from her. But she didn't see it.

As a result, the teachers at Fern Street Elementary School decided to harvest wins for each other. They committed to visit classrooms and specifically name things that the teacher did to improve students' learning. This was intentional and purposeful on their part. As a first-grade teacher noted, "I think we're all in Ms. Greene's shoes. We're not sure that we're having an impact and we're not sure how to tell. But when another teacher told me that my video lesson on adding numbers was really impacting students' learning, I was thrilled. But I asked how she knew, and she said that she saw students teaching each other. She said they could explain all of the steps and they were using the words 'addends' and 'sum.' Amazing. Wow. I said to myself, *It's working. They are learning.*"

REFLECT

How can you harvest wins? What success stories are you capturing and how are you attributing effort to those successes? Are you doing this for yourself? And are you doing this for others?

SPRING FORWARD

Educator efficacy and agency are important in the success of schools. In this module, we have focused on you as an individual. We recognize the power of the collective as well as the fact that collective efficacy is dependent, in large part, on individual efficacy and agency. If you are not feeling effective or do not think that your efforts are impacting your students, it's hard to want to be part of a team. And it's hard to think that the work of the team matters when your own work does not seem to matter. To rebound from these pandemics, we need to rebuild our individual efficacy and agency. As we will discuss later, this will allows us to also build the power of the collective.

REFLECT

Reflect on your learning about efficacy and agency and their impact on you, your sense of success, and the satisfaction you receive from work. Identify actions you are considering based on your learning.

IMPORTANT

On a scale of 1 to 5, with 5 being very important and 1 being not important at all, how would you rate the value of efficacy and agency in your classroom or school?

1   2   3   4   5

WAIT, BUT WHY?

Explain your reason for the rating above.

MODULE 3

REBUILDING STUDENT AGENCY

Agency isn't just for adults. Young people's sense of agency drives their learning in and out of school. You can see a student's agency in your own classroom. The students who exhibit self-regulation skills such as taking turns and working through a multistep math problem draw on their agency. The metacognition needed to reflect on ideas, ask questions, and recognize their progress is another dimension of agency in learning. Those two elements—self-regulation and metacognition—fuel learning. The school years are essential, as self-regulation and metacognition undergo rapid development beginning at about four years of age and continuing across a lifetime.

Student agency is key to our success as educators. Teaching is not a push-and-pull process, with the teacher pushing information out and the student pulling the information in. Think of student agency as the catalyst that makes those exchanges possible.

The agency of many young people has taken a hit during remote learning. There has been a destabilizing effect for some students who do not see the fruits of their labors. Decreased socialization opportunities with peers haven't helped, and some of the cues that are in a physical classroom have been harder to come by. Rebuilding student agency is crucial to re-establishing their relationship to learning.

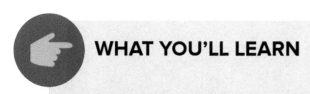

WHAT YOU'LL LEARN

LEARNING INTENTIONS

- I am learning about eight dimensions of student agency.

- I am learning about creating student opportunities to rebuild student agency.

- I am learning about the role of student collaboration in agency.

- I am learning about teacher-led approaches to build student agency.

SUCCESS CRITERIA

- I can create a plan to embed student agency in my classroom or school.

- I can host individual conferences with students about their agency.

- I can utilize feedback to build agency and motivation.

- I can help students reestablish their relationship with learning.

SELF-ASSESSMENT

Use the provided scale to identify your level of knowledge about student agency. Consider each of these statements:

- I am knowledgeable about the role of student agency in learning.

- I know specific ways to build student agency in my classroom.

- I understand how goal setting can fuel student agency.

- I am aware of how feedback can build student agency.

RE-ESTABLISHING A RELATIONSHIP TO LEARNING

There is much to celebrate about what our students have learned to do in this past school year. The rise in their digital competency (and our own) is extraordinary. Young children have learned how to take screenshots and create short videos explaining their thinking. Older students navigate learning management systems (LMS) like the pros they have become. Many young people have learned a new level of time management that is less dependent on bells and schedules (talk about self-regulation!).

But much has been lost as well, especially in terms of students' relationship to learning. Learning is an inherently social act, typically constructed with other humans (Vygotsky, 1978). Our students have had to navigate a learning landscape they were not prepared for (not just an LMS). In the absence of the environmental cues of the classroom, many had to reconcile learning in a home environment more readily associated with sleeping, eating, or play. Because the teacher wasn't able to use proximity, gestural cues, and physical prompts like a hand on a shoulder to redirect, caregivers had to run interference instead. Shortened instructional minutes meant that there was a greater reliance on independent learning, but with less supervision and encouragement than comes when it is happening in a live space.

REBUILDING STUDENT AGENCY IS CRUCIAL TO RE-ESTABLISHING THEIR RELATIONSHIP TO LEARNING.

Those who lack the skills of agency about their learning are likely to suffer the most from pandemic teaching. On the other hand, we can learn much to reboot our classrooms from enhanced attention to teaching self-regulation skills, having students less dependent on us, and devising lesson planning to capitalize on students teaching and learning from each other.

The cost to student agency has been greater still for vulnerable students. It is a double-whammy. Many experienced economic hardships and lack of reliable access to the internet. Others had difficulty in carving out a figurative and literal learning space in households stretched thin by childcare, unemployment, sickness, and, in some cases, substance abuse. Children and their families found themselves unhoused, crushed by racial injustices, and weathering the profound loss and death of loved ones. Students with disabilities, English learners, and others who require compensatory supports had fewer options, despite the efforts of schools and districts.

It's fair to say that the confidence of many learners has been shaken by the experiences they have had during the past year. Young people are amazingly resilient, and without question, all of us continue to be awed by what students have and still are accomplishing. There are many who flourished with the reduced teacher direction, the bells, the distractions of others, and the opportunity to be efficient in their learning. They certainly should not be forced to go back to the old ways and lose these values and skills. We have a rebuilding process in front of us. We need to re-establish students' relationship to learning.

PAUSE & PONDER

Consider the experiences you believe your students had or may continue to be having that could be a threat to their sense of agency.

1. **My students are/were able to regularly access technology (hardware and internet).**

None (0%–10%)　　　Some (11%–50%)　　　Most (51%–89%)　　　All (90%–100%)

2. **My students have/have had difficulty in finding a reliable physical space to learn.**

None (0%–10%)　　　Some (11%–50%)　　　Most (51%–89%)　　　All (90%–100%)

3. **The families of my students are/were able to provide consistent learning support.**

None (0%–10%)　　　Some (11%–50%)　　　Most (51%–89%)　　　All (90%–100%)

4. **My students are/have experienced housing and/or food insecurity.**

None (0%–10%)　　　Some (11%–50%)　　　Most (51%–89%)　　　All (90%–100%)

5. **My students have/had significant attendance problems that compromised their learning.**

None (0%–10%)　　　Some (11%–50%)　　　Most (51%–89%)　　　All (90%–100%)

6. **My students are/were able to access compensatory supports at pre-pandemic levels (special education, language, counseling, or tutoring supports).**

None (0%–10%)　　　Some (11%–50%)　　　Most (51%–89%)　　　All (90%–100%)

7. **My students are/were able to complete independent work.**

None (0%–10%)　　　Some (11%–50%)　　　Most (51%–89%)　　　All (90%–100%)

8. **My students are/were able to collaborate with their peers.**

None (0%–10%)　　　Some (11%–50%)　　　Most (51%–89%)　　　All (90%–100%)

EIGHT DIMENSIONS OF STUDENT AGENCY

Agency is central to a positive relationship to learning. Student agency is the management of one's own learning. Students with low levels of agency believe that learning is something that happens to them, and if they don't learn something, it is because of the teacher's inadequacies or their own traits. They don't see their own role in their learning. Dominique's daughter asked him to throw the ball to her. When she didn't catch it, she said, "You missed." She attributed her lack of success to him.

Student agency is multidimensional and fostered by approaches to instruction, task design, motivation, assessment, and the development of study habits. These are also key for transfer of learning, which is the ability to apply knowledge and strategies under new conditions (National Research Council, 2012). Research on student agency in schools identified eight dimensions: self-efficacy, pursuit of interest, perseverance of effort, locus of control, mastery orientation, metacognition, future orientation, and self-regulation (Zeiser et al., 2018).

STUDENTS WITH LOW LEVELS OF AGENCY BELIEVE THAT LEARNING IS SOMETHING THAT HAPPENS TO THEM.

Self-efficacy. The belief that one can achieve goals is fundamental to student agency, as it is with adults. You'll recall from the previous module that the four sources of self-efficacy are having mastery experiences, seeing models, benefiting from social persuasion and encouragement, and knowing how to manage the physiological responses (Bandura, 1982). A child who possesses a higher level of self-efficacy believes that they can reach goals. Self-efficacy, with an effect size of 0.71, reliably holds the potential to accelerate learning (Hattie, n.d.; www.visiblelearningmexta.com).

Pursuit of interest. Think of this as a consistency of passion for a topic. We've seen the determination of students to learn everything there is to know about something that has seized their interest: coding, the Titanic disaster, geocaching, ice skating. They pursue their interests by reading books, talking with others about them, practice, and searching for new challenges that will build their skills. An important aspect of this is that they stick with some interests for a period of time and don't lose interest quickly (Peña & Duckworth, 2018).

Perseverance of effort. Hand-in-hand with interest is the willingness to continue on when something becomes more difficult. A student's persistence and concentration of effort to finish tasks has the potential to accelerate learning, with an effect size of 0.54 (Hattie, n.d.; www.visiblelearningmexta.com). A student with a higher degree of persistence understands that setbacks can happen but is willing to see a project or task through to the end. Importantly, perseverance of effort can't be fostered when the tasks are not challenging. Unfortunately, this happens too often with some advanced students who skate through their years of schooling, only to discover that when they reach college, they don't have the wherewithal or the resiliency to confront challenge.

Locus of control. The key word is "control"—To what extent does a learner believe that they are an influencer in the successful completion of the task? The location, or locus, of control speaks to where they attribute success and failure. A person with a strong internal locus of control places a higher value on their own skills and effort, while those with an external locus of control focus on the difficulty of the project or what other people's skill levels are. In truth, locus of control is on a continuum, rather than an internal/external binary. Learners can also attribute luck or an authority, such as the teacher, in explaining their success. A learner who says, "The teacher doesn't like me; that's why I got a bad grade" is attributing failure to an external authority figure. "I got lucky on that exam, so that's why I got a good grade" is attributing success to luck. An internal locus of control is associated with higher levels of achievement (Shepherd et al., 2006).

Mastery orientation. Goals drive all of us, but there is also the motivation for those goals. The beliefs we have about the goal orient us onto a path. The goals of students can fall broadly into two paths: a mastery orientation or a performance orientation (Pintrich, 2003). Students with a mastery orientation understand that what they are learning benefits them. They understand that learning a topic in one class will benefit them in another. As well, they judge their own performance in terms of what they have learned, not in comparison to others. A student with a mastery orientation says, "I want to learn Spanish so I can speak to my grandparents." Students with a performance orientation have goals, too, but they may be tied more closely to the amount of effort required and their standing with others. A student with a performance orientation may say, "I want to pass Spanish class" or "I want to get an A in this class so I can move up in the class ranking." A student with a deep motivation and approach seeks mastery and is willing to invest a higher degree of effort. That kind of motivation has an effect size of 0.57 and can accelerate learning (Hattie, n.d.; www.visiblelearningmetax.com), which is why we encourage conversations with students about the question, "Why are we learning this?"

Metacognition. Often described as "thinking about thinking," metacognition develops in the first years of schooling and continues across a lifetime. You'll notice this happening with the five-year-old that checks the picture on a puzzle box lid to complete it. Metacognitive strategies are embedded in instruction. We teach early readers to monitor their understanding so that when they lose meaning in a text, they go back to reread. We teach older students to take notes and use them as part of their studying. A student with a higher degree of metacognition will notice what is confusing, ask questions, and mentally summarize what they are learning.

A CHILD WHO POSSESSES A HIGHER LEVEL OF SELF-EFFICACY BELIEVES THAT THEY CAN REACH GOALS.

MODULE 3

Future orientation. Perceptions of what constitutes the future are definitely going to vary with age. Young children may consider the future to be lunchtime. But a goal of schooling is to help students see that the learning they do today is grounded not only in their current context but also in their investment in their own future aspirations. Early grades social studies curriculum includes study of different occupations and community roles, and lots of schools host Career Days so that children can ask questions about how the firefighter decided on that professional field. Middle and high school efforts include helping students develop resumes and introducing academic and extracurricular efforts that will burnish their postsecondary applications. Students with a future orientation are able to equate their school efforts and experiences as a foundation for adult aspirations.

Self-regulation. All of these above relate to the notion of "self-regulation," a term closely related to metacognition. A student with a higher degree of self-regulation can reset their attention during math when they notice they're thinking instead about a video game; they can choose a different strategy for learning when the first does not work; they can seek, hear, and act on feedback from others. Self-regulation plays an important role in practice and studying. For instance, being organized, keeping track of assignments, and setting aside time for study are all essential skills.

CASE IN POINT

Lynette Carter and Randy Espinoza are educators who share several students in common. Mr. Espinoza is the special educator who supports the English department at their inclusive high school, and Ms. Carter is one of the English teachers. They are hosting individual meetings with some students who have been a cause of concern because of what they perceive as a lack of agency, damaging their relationship to learning. They don't want these conversations to devolve into a litany of problems, the shaking of an adult finger, and a silent and sullen teen. Instead, they use a scripted series of questions to talk to each student (Smith et al., 2015):

1. When do you feel proud of yourself, inside or outside of school?

2. Why did you feel that way?

3. What obstacles did you overcome, and how did you do it?

4. What obstacle is holding you back right now?

5. Could some of those same strategies you used to overcome obstacles be used in this situation?

6. Let's make a plan to overcome that obstacle. I bet you're already feeling proud of yourself for tackling this.

THE AMOUNT OF AUTONOMY EXPERIENCED BY STUDENTS HAS A DIRECT LINK TO THEIR SENSE OF AGENCY.

Arturo is one of the students they are meeting with today. He transferred to the school before the pandemic as an eleventh-grade student who was behind in his credits and eligible for special education services. A transcript analysis meant that he needed to enroll in some classes that are typically completed in tenth grade, and while it was a blow to his ego, he made steady progress and recouped some of his earlier losses. However, his return to school has been problematic. He struggled with distance learning and has not made expected gains in face-to-face instruction. His family was hit hard by COVID-19 and his father nearly lost his life after weeks on a ventilator. As the oldest child, Arturo took care of his family during the crisis.

REFLECT

What do you see as strengths to leverage to rebuild Arturo's sense of agency? Which dimensions of agency would you suggest these educators target (keep in mind that they can target more than one)?

TEACHER PRACTICES TO REBUILD STUDENT AGENCY

Teachers play an important role in the relative amount of agency a student possesses. You'll recall that we discussed teacher autonomy in Module 1. The amount of autonomy experienced by students has a direct link to their sense of agency (Filippello et al., 2019). Teaching that is highly controlling places a premium on compliance, conveys approval that is dependent on achievement, and ignores students who do not achieve, resulting in a "chilly" classroom climate. These teaching behaviors foster an external locus of control that is authority based, and students in these classrooms grow more insecure about their learning and their ability to take action. The result can often be learned helplessness.

In contrast, teaching styles that increase students' autonomy foster those who have a higher sense of learning agency (Filippello et al., 2019). These autonomy-supportive classrooms are led by teachers who encourage discussion, listen for students' points of view, make feedback informative, and take the time to link student actions to their success. Choice and relevance are crucial curricular

MODULE 3

features. Importantly, in doing so, they help students develop an internal locus of control. For a student who has had a compromised relationship to learning, autonomy-supportive classrooms can be transformative.

We note a problem in that it is students who perform above average who prefer teachers taking more control, talking more, asking more about the facts—as they know how to play this game and are winners. Many forms of our current accountability systems are dependent on multiple-choice or closed forms of assessment. These appear to students to privilege content-based knowledge, and so often these students come to believe that the "good student" is the one who "knows lots." It is fascinating to note how few gifted students go onto become gifted adults (less than 2% of child prodigies do so) primarily, we would argue, as they do not have high skills at self-regulation in areas other than their "gift," struggle with not knowing, fear challenges in areas where they are less familiar, and have fewer skills of working in teams to solve problems (often preferring to shine by themselves).

> FOR A STUDENT WHO HAS HAD A COMPROMISED RELATIONSHIP TO LEARNING, AUTONOMY-SUPPORTIVE CLASSROOMS CAN BE TRANSFORMATIVE.

The intentional use of teacher practices specifically aimed at building student agency has shown promising results over time, as short as within a single school year (Zeiser et al., 2018). Given that the rebuilding of student agency can fuel student learning, this is an investment that can deliver measurable results. In this module and those that follow, we will discuss these practices, which cluster into three categories: student opportunities, student–teacher collaboration, and teacher-led approaches. How many of these practices are part of your daily instruction?

PAUSE & PONDER

Menu of Teacher Practices on Student Agency

Use the traffic light scale to reflect on your current practices as they relate to teaching about and creating opportunities for agency. What areas do you want to strengthen?

STUDENT OPPORTUNITIES

Choice. Students make choices about their strategies for learning.	
Group work. Students have opportunities to work in groups to learn and practice agency necessary for group success.	
Harnessing outside opportunities. Students have opportunities to demonstrate agency outside the classroom and make connections to its application in the classroom.	

STUDENT OPPORTUNITIES (Continued)

Revision. Students are able to revise assignments or tests after they receive feedback.

Student self-reflection. Students self-reflect using journals, logs, or other structured templates or tools.

Student-led instruction. Students demonstrate agency by leading instruction on a particular skill or concept.

STUDENT–TEACHER COLLABORATION

Developing relationships. Teachers develop personal relationships with students to better understand their agency strengths, needs, and motivators.

Feedback. Teachers provide students with feedback and scaffold the process of students seeking feedback.

Goal setting. Teachers help students set goals to complete coursework while improving agency.

Individual conferences. Teachers hold one-on-one meetings with students to discuss elements of student agency and its relationship to academic work.

Student voice. Teachers provide students with opportunities to contribute to and provide feedback on key decisions in the classroom.

TEACHER-LED APPROACHES

Assessment. Teachers design ways to evaluate student learning agency.

Direct instruction. Teachers provide explicit instruction to develop skills related to student agency.

Modeling. Teachers model agency to demonstrate it to students in a meaningful context.

Positive reinforcement. Teachers provide positive reinforcement for demonstration of agency.

Scaffolding. Teachers provide students with tools, strategies, and resources to help scaffold students toward mastery of agency.

Verbal cues. Teachers provide brief spoken prompts in real time to highlight or remind students of behaviors that demonstrate agency.

MODULE 3

Source: Adapted from Zeiser, K., Scholz, C., & Cirks, V. (2018). *Maximizing student agency: Implementing and measuring student-centered learning practices* (Appendix A: Menu of Teacher Practices on Student Agency). American Institutes of Research. https://files.eric.ed.gov/fulltext/ED592084.pdf

THREE WAYS TO CHANGE THE RELATIONSHIP TO LEARNING BEGINNING TOMORROW

Increased student agency doesn't occur due to a few isolated practices that happen every once in a while. The steady implementation of the techniques discussed in the previous "Pause and Ponder" requires commitment on your part. It's important to gain a toehold to ramp up your practice. We'll take one element from each of the three areas of the teaching practices for student agency scale to build a foundation.

1. Student Opportunities for Self-Reflection and Self-Assessment

Do you know that feeling when you are trying to make your way through a dark and unfamiliar room? Your senses are heightened as you strain to see and hear, hoping for a clue. You move slowly and cautiously for fear you'll run into something or even fall. But switch the light on, and you visibly relax as you move with more assurance. Student self-reflection works like a light—it illuminates a path that makes acceleration possible.

STUDENT SELF-REFLECTION WORKS LIKE A LIGHT—IT ILLUMINATES A PATH THAT MAKES ACCELERATION POSSIBLE.

Students need opportunities to regularly reflect on their progress. This builds their confidence, allows them to make plans for improvement, and reinforces their awareness of their skills (a metacognitive trait). Further, these should happen through the learning process. At the beginning of a unit of instruction, share the success criteria for the students and allow them to rank order the relative level of difficulty for each item. Although this is in advance of instruction, it provides students with an opportunity to consider their own present skill level and to make early decisions about where they will need to concentrate more effort. The feedback to you is quite helpful, too. Imagine knowing at the start of a unit who already is feeling as though they may have more difficulty than you anticipated. This presents opportunities to provide instruction on gaps in skills or concepts, as well as to provide students with feedback about their agency. Figure 2 displays an example of a seventh-grade math unit on multiplying and dividing rational numbers; notice how this particular student said that identifying a terminating or repeating decimal would probably be the most difficult.

A second technique for prompting self-reflection about progress is to compare assessments over a period of time. This type of assessment, called ipsative assessment, is used to compare a student's past performance to a current one (Isaacs et al., 2013). Teachers often do ipsative evaluation to gauge growth over time, but it is less common for students to do so. This process allows the student to notice where growth has occurred and is self-referential (*How did I do compared to six weeks ago?*) rather than peer-oriented (*How did I do compared to my classmates?*). You see young children delight in doing this when they

Figure 2 Sample Self-Ranking of Success Criteria

Difficulty	Success Criteria
3	I can use properties of operations to multiply and divide rational numbers.
5	I can identify the decimal form of a rational number as a terminating or repeating decimal.
4	I can convert a rational number to a decimal using long division.
2	I can justify the quotients of rational numbers.
1	I can justify the products of rational numbers.

compare a drawing they did at age three to another they made at age six. These comparative self-assessments can be especially motivating for learners who have larger attainment gaps compared to the grade-level expectations, as it allows them to view their growth and developmental progress (Hughes et al., 2014). Figure 3 is an example of an ipsative assessment about writing. The student chooses two pieces of writing, comparing one from earlier in the semester to a more recent one to identify where they have grown and where to focus effort.

Figure 3 Comparative Self-Assessment for Informational Writing in Grade 6

Title and Date of First Essay	Title and Date of Second Essay
Organization/Purpose	
Topic is introduced clearly to preview what is to follow 4 3 2 1	Topic is introduced clearly to preview what is to follow 4 3 2 1
Ideas and concepts are organized using definition, classification, or compare/contrast 4 3 2 1	Ideas and concepts are organized using definition, classification, or compare/contrast 4 3 2 1
Transitions create cohesion and show relationships among ideas 4 3 2 1	Transitions create cohesion and show relationships among ideas 4 3 2 1
A concluding statement supports the explanation given 4 3 2 1	A concluding statement supports the explanation given 4 3 2 1
Task, purpose, and audience are aligned to prompt 4 3 2 1	Task, purpose, and audience are aligned to prompt 4 3 2 1
Evidence/Elaboration	
Develops the topic with relevant facts, definitions, details, and examples 4 3 2 1	Develops the topic with relevant facts, definitions, details, and examples 4 3 2 1
Follows a standard format for citations 4 3 2 1	Follows a standard format for citations 4 3 2 1

(Continued)

(Continued)

Evidence/Elaboration (Continued)							
Skillfully quotes and paraphrases				Skillfully quotes and paraphrases			
4	3	2	1	4	3	2	1
Uses relevant information from multiple sources				Uses relevant information from multiple sources			
4	3	2	1	4	3	2	1
Effective and appropriate style enhances content				Effective and appropriate style enhances content			
4	3	2	1	4	3	2	1
Conventions							
Demonstrates grade-level grammar, usage, and conventions				Demonstrates grade-level grammar, usage, and conventions			
4	3	2	1	4	3	2	1

Source: Fisher, D., Frey, N., Bustamante, V., & Hattie, J. (2021). *The assessment playbook for distance and blended learning.* Corwin.

PAUSE & PONDER

How Do Your Students Self-Reflect and Self-Assess?

There are many other ways to build these habits with your students. How many of these do you currently use?

SELF-REFLECTION	YES	NO	SELF-ASSESSMENT	YES	NO
I ask self-reflection questions at the end of assignments.			I use anticipation guides at the beginning of units so that students can identify their background knowledge.		
I ask self-reflection questions at the end of quizzes and tests.			I use polls or other universal response techniques so that students can self-assess.		
I have students make short videos of their reflections.			I have students compare their work to a rubric or checklist to self-assess before submitting it.		
I ask students to write exit slips at the end of lessons.			I provide time after collaborative tasks for students to debrief their processes.		

What self-reflection and self-assessment tools might you add to your repertoire?

2. Student–Teacher Collaboration for Goal Setting

Build the habits of self-reflection and self-assessment and you'll open the door to goal setting. A second aspect of rebuilding student agency is to assist them in setting goals. These can be academic goals for the completion of course work but can be further strengthened by imbuing them with agency. For example, a goal to "get better grades" is not especially useful—it is vague, doesn't have a time limit, lacks details in terms of the student tracking their progress, and, worst of all in terms of agency, doesn't have any kind of action plan to go with it. Solid goals meet four conditions (Martin, 2006):

- Specific in nature

- Challenging to the student

- Competitively self-referenced

- Based on self-improvement

We are fans of a personal-best approach to goal setting (Martin, 2006). These growth-oriented goals are set by the student to improve on previous performance. An important element shouldn't be lost—these are goals set by the student, not by someone else. They can be outcome goals, such as "improve my comprehension skills so I can achieve a new benchmark in my reading level," or process oriented, such as reading for fifteen minutes every evening. Notice that neither of these goals involves comparisons to others; they have mastery, rather than performance, in mind. Because the goal is co-constructed with the student, personal-best goals are associated with higher levels of intrinsic motivation, persistence, engagement, and enjoyment of school (Martin, 2011). Goals set with students can be personal (try out for the swim team) or nonacademic but school related (attendance).

DON'T GET DISCOURAGED IF THEIR INITIAL GOALS DON'T SEEM ALL THAT SUBSTANTIAL. YOU ARE BUILDING A HABIT AND A DISPOSITION FOR THEM.

Strengthen their personal link to the goal by discussing why it is of value to them. Too often young people will go through a goal-setting exercise because there is an adult insisting on it. When you talk with them about why it is important to them (not school, family, or friends), you further foster their sense of agency about the decisions they make and the direction they choose. Don't get discouraged if their initial goals don't seem all that substantial. You are building a habit and a disposition for them. Regaining one's agency takes time and it also takes early and small wins.

Importantly, it isn't so much the initial goal setting that has an effect, but rather what is done with it. If a goal is set but never revisited, it holds little to no value. Check in regularly with students to discuss their progress and adjust their planned actions as needed. Knowing that their plans can be adjusted based on new circumstances can be an eye-opener for students. They often look at the adults in their lives and see the accomplishments, but not all the zigzags it took to get there. These conferences are a great time to share your story and struggles and, in the process, build a relationship. And keep in mind what Bandura (1982) said

MODULE 3

about self-efficacy: there is incredible value in seeing agency modeled. But they'll never know how you have used your own agency if all they see are the outcomes, not the path you took to get there. An example of a personal goal-setting conference is in Figure 4.

Figure 4   Planning Tool for a Personal-Best Goal-Setting Conference

What is an academic, school-related, or personal goal you have for yourself?

- Why is this something you value?

- What has your past performance been like? What has been your personal best so far?

- How will achieving this goal benefit you?

- How will you know you have been successful?

- What might get in the way of you meeting this goal?

- What do you need to achieve this goal?

Resources	Self	School	Family

Action steps to achieve this goal:

1.

2.

3.

We will check in with each other every _____ weeks to talk about your progress toward your personal-best goal.

3. Teacher-Led Positive Reinforcement That Motivates

"If you're going to offer critique, focus on the process and the possibility," said Johnston (2012, p. 37). The language you use, he noted, shapes the agency that learners possess about their ability to act on the world. Noting that "causal statements are at the heart of building agency," he and others have found that the power of feedback lies in its potential learning forward. Feedback that is general and vague is not going to build much agency or, for that matter, close the gap between their current level of performance and where they're headed. Telling a student "Good job!" is not especially motivating. Making progress is highly motivating. The quality of the feedback offered can be motivating for students, particularly when it is useful for the student.

There are four types of feedback: task related, process related, self-regulation related, and feedback about the person (Hattie & Timperley, 2007). Corrective feedback about the task (correct/not correct) has an important potential to motivate as students are beginning to learn the subject matter, the vocabulary of the task, and the basic ideas. Often such corrective feedback can be followed by re-teaching to ensure students have these basics before they move to relational and conceptual thinking. We do note that much of the written feedback we offer to students is in this form, and indeed students often welcome this form of feedback—as it is relatively easier to amend than deeper, more conceptual thinking. But we need to be careful that we do not stay with task feedback, as doing so reinforces to students that this is the prime purpose of the lesson.

TELLING A STUDENT "GOOD JOB!" IS NOT ESPECIALLY MOTIVATING. MAKING PROGRESS IS HIGHLY MOTIVATING.

Feedback about process and self-regulation holds a higher potential to motivate deeper thinking and mastery. In terms of process, drawing a student's attention to something they successfully used reinforces elements of the process you want them to continue using. Adding the phrase "look how you" to process can be a game changer (Johnston, 2012).

- "Look how you mixed colors to paint the sky."
- "Look how you worked with your peers in the shared doc and figured out this problem."
- "Look how you used a math model to help you figure out this problem."
- "Look how you thought about Boyle's law when you were calculating pressure."
- "Look how you shared your video reflection with the class."

Mind you, all of these can be followed with further feedback about what might have caused an error. Feedback about process is especially useful in helping students detect errors (Hattie & Timperley, 2007):

- "Look how you mixed colors to paint the sky. How could you use that same technique for the mountain lake in your painting?"

- "Look how you worked with your peers in the shared doc and figured out this problem. How can you use that experience to solve a problem on your own?"

- "Look how you used a math model to help you figure out this problem. Can you look at that model again to see what might have led you to the incorrect answer?"

- "Look how you thought about Boyle's law when you were calculating pressure. Why didn't it work as well when you were calculating the volume?"

- "Look how you shared your video reflection with the class. Can you work on your self-assessment and identify areas of strength and one area to grow?"

A second feedback technique is about self-regulation. This approach holds the possibility of being motivating for students. It can be the difference between the "want to do" element of motivation versus the negative feedback that can lead to "have to do" (Hattie & Timperley, 2007, p. 99). Feedback about self-regulation speaks in particular to agency:

- "I noticed that when the clay started wobbling on the potter's wheel, you didn't get frustrated and you kept going. How did that feel?"

- "I can see by your chart that you're logging at least fifteen minutes a night reading. You're keeping yourself focused even when there are other things you could be doing. What has been getting easier for you to do that?"

- "You were listening carefully to your opponent during the debate. Did that help you form your counterargument?"

Positive reinforcement about agency is crucial for students, as it assists them in seeing the results of their actions. Pair your feedback with a question that invites the student to self-reinforce (Zeiser et al., 2018). You want students to see their own growing agency:

- "I don't get frustrated."

- "I don't get distracted."

- "I listen instead of just arguing back."

After all, the product of agency is how we talk to ourselves about our capacity to take action.

Feedback directed to the person tends to get recalled, as we all love to hear praise, what a wonderful person we are, and are hurt when the comments about us are negative. The power of these emotions so often leads to the student not then hearing the feedback about the work. Praise tends to dilute the impact of feedback on learning and achievement. This does not mean you should not use praise (it can be the essence of building positive relations), but we invite you to separate the occasions when you praise—and not include praise when you are providing feedback about the task, processes, or self-regulation.

CASE IN POINT

The teaching staff at Fair Haven Elementary School have returned to face-to-face instruction after a prolonged period of virtual learning. Their students have done pretty well academically, and the families in their school have had praise for the school's efforts to keep their children connected to school and each other. In anticipation of returning, the school's instructional leadership team met with the parent–teacher organization to set some broad goals to be accomplished this year. One of them is to develop a schoolwide plan to rebuild student agency.

REFLECT

How would you advise Fair Haven to proceed? What kinds of tangible actions could they take to build a student agency initiative? We've reproduced items from the earlier assessment in this module to spark your thinking.

STUDENT OPPORTUNITIES	STUDENT–TEACHER COLLABORATION	TEACHER-LED APPROACHES
Choice	Developing relationships	Assessment
Group work	Feedback	Direct instruction
Harnessing outside opportunities	Goal setting	Modeling
Revision	Individual conferences	Positive reinforcement
Student self-reflection	Student voice	Scaffolding
Student-led instruction		Verbal cues

POSSIBLE ACTIONS

SPRING FORWARD

Student agency fuels learning. During COVID times, many students have likely experienced some loss of agency about their learning and their lives, compromising their relationship with learning. Their agency hinges on two important elements: self-regulation and metacognition. If we are to make strides in addressing learning recovery, then we must take agency head on. Rebuilding agency is something we can do through the actions we take. First, we must talk about agency with our students—not just as a stand-alone lesson but as an ongoing conversation. We need to extend agency by creating opportunities for students to learn about themselves, notice their actions, and understand the goals they have for themselves, not just the ones that well-meaning adults have for them. Finally, we need to embed agency into the encouragement and feedback we offer to our students. That's a goal for every educator: How are my actions building the agency of others?

REFLECT

Reflect on your learning about agency and its impact on students' learning. Identify actions you are considering based on your learning.

IMPORTANT

On a scale of 1 to 5, with 5 being very important and 1 being not important at all, how would you rate the value of addressing the student agency and rebuilding students' relationship with learning?

1   2   3   4   5

WAIT, BUT WHY?

Explain your reason for the rating above.

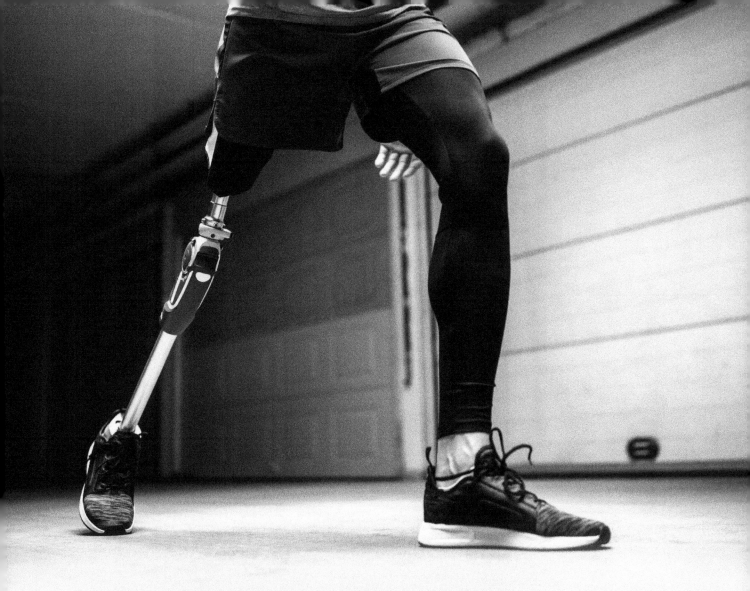

MODULE 4

RECOVERING LEARNING THROUGH CURRICULUM

Educators make decisions about what to teach (the curriculum), how to teach it (the instruction), and how to know what students have learned (the assessments). These three areas influence the decisions we make and the outcomes we get. These major levers did not change during distance learning and they still exist as we begin to rebound from the pandemics.

What did change is the ways in which we think about the curriculum, new ways for engaging students in instruction, and how to best know if students have learned. In fact, we have learned a lot over the past year that can be used to improve the experiences students have in school.

We should acknowledge that these three areas—curriculum, instruction, and assessment—are deeply linked together, and it's hard to talk about one without thinking about the others. But, for purposes of addressing learning recovery, it seems reasonable to dissect each of these areas and consider the ways in which we can recover the learning students need to do.

When it comes to curriculum, our first area to address learning recovery, it's important to know the expectations for a grade level or subject area. It's also important to know where students are in their learning journey. See, we've already treaded into assessment. Back to curriculum, to address learning recovery, it's valuable to identify key standards that students must master while also addressing the unfinished learning that students may have. And that's going to take some organizing and coordinating.

WHAT YOU'LL LEARN

LEARNING INTENTIONS

- I am learning about learning recovery.

- I am learning about the ways in which curriculum can support learning recovery.

SUCCESS CRITERIA

- I can analyze the expectations I hold for students.

- I can analyze standards and identify appropriate learning expectations.

- I can identify content and skills that my students have already mastered.

- I can negotiate priority learning for my students.

- I can design challenging tasks based on students' learning needs.

SELF-ASSESSMENT

Using the provided scale, identify your level of knowledge about addressing learning recovery through the curriculum. Consider each of these statements:

- I am aware of the expectations I hold for students.

- I understand the characteristics of high expectations.

- I analyze standards to identify concepts and skills.

- I develop learning intentions and success criteria.

(Continued)

(Continued)

- I design initial assessment to determine my students' prior knowledge and skills.

- I am aware of priority learning that my students need to accomplish this year.

- The tasks I design are challenging for students and aligned with appropriate standards.

TEACHER EXPECTATIONS FOR STUDENT LEARNING

There is a saying attributed to the Persian poet Hafiz that "the words you use are the house you live in." If we believe that there is widespread loss of learning, and that is what we talk about, our tendency is to look for gaps. To close those gaps, we focus on remediation. In doing so, we slow down learning and give ourselves permission to lower expectations. As the logic goes, there is a large gap due to the learning loss, and thus we cannot expect as much this year (or the next, or the next). The language of learning loss becomes the house we live in. We do not believe that teachers intentionally lower their expectations, but rather that the narrative about learning loss leads to it. It is deficit thinking. And students do not win when their teachers engage in deficit thinking.

What if, instead, we accept that there was an impact from the experiences of the pandemics and focus our efforts on acceleration and recovery of learning? What if we talk about learning leaps instead of learning loss? What if we identify where students are in their learning and identify critical content that they must learn now to accelerate their performance in the future? And what if we raise our expectations for students rather than lower them? We see tremendous potential with this shift in thinking. After all, teacher expectations have an effect size of 0.43, slightly above the average of all influences on learning. Let's agree not to reduce the impact that our expectations have on students' learning.

Teachers who have high expectations believe that the students they teach will make accelerated growth, not simply "normal" progress (Rubie-Davies, 2014).

Teachers with lower expectations assign tasks that are less cognitively demanding, spend time repeating information over and over again, focus on classroom rules and procedures, and accept a lower standard of work (Rubie-Davies, 2008). As summarized in the education hub (Hood, 2020), high expectation teachers

- Communicate learning intentions and success criteria with the class
- Ask more open questions, designed to extend or enhance students' thinking by requiring them to think more deeply
- Manage behavior positively and proactively
- Make more positive statements and create a positive class climate
- Set specific goals with students that are regularly reviewed and used for teaching and learning
- Take a facilitative role and support students to make choices about their learning
- Link achievement to motivation, effort, and goal setting
- Encourage students to work with a variety of peers for positive peer modeling
- Provide less differentiation and allow all learners to engage in advanced activities
- Undertake more assessment and monitoring so that students' learning strategies can be adjusted when necessary
- Work with all students equally
- Give specific, instructional feedback about students' achievement in relation to learning goals
- Respond to incorrect answers by exploring the wrong answer, rephrasing explanations, or scaffolding the student to the correct answer
- Base learning opportunities around students' interests for motivation (p. 4)

WE DO NOT BELIEVE THAT TEACHERS INTENTIONALLY LOWER THEIR EXPECTATIONS, BUT RATHER THAT THE NARRATIVE ABOUT LEARNING LOSS LEADS TO IT.

PAUSE & PONDER

Use the following self-assessment checklist to identify the frequency of the high expectation practices that you use.

HOW OFTEN DO YOU USE THE FOLLOWING HIGH EXPECTATION PRACTICES IN YOUR TEACHING?	RARELY	SOMETIMES	OFTEN
Ask open questions			
Praise effort rather than correct answers			
Use regular formative assessment			

(Continued)

(Continued)

HOW OFTEN DO YOU USE THE FOLLOWING HIGH EXPECTATION PRACTICES IN YOUR TEACHING?	RARELY	SOMETIMES	OFTEN
Rephrase questions when answers are incorrect			
Use mixed-ability groupings			
Change groupings regularly			
Encourage students to work with a range of their peers			
Provide a range of activities			
Allow students to choose their own activities from a range of options			
Make explicit learning intentions and success criteria			
Allow students to contribute to success criteria			
Give students responsibility for their learning			
Get to know each student personally			
Incorporate students' interests into activities			
Establish routines and procedures at the beginning of the school year			
Work with students to set individual goals			
Teach students about SMART (specific, measurable, achievable, realistic, and timely) goals			
Regularly review goals with students			
Link achievement to motivation, effort, and goal setting			
Minimize differentiation in activities between high and low achievers			
Allow all learners to engage in advanced activities			
Give specific, instructional feedback about students' achievement in relation to learning goals			
Take a facilitative role and support students to make choices about their learning			
Manage behavior positively and proactively			
Work with all students equally			

Source: Hargraves, V. (2018). High expectations self assessment checklist. How to develop high expectation teaching. The Education Hub. https://theeducationhub.org.nz/how-to-develop-high-expectations-teaching. Developed from Rubie-Davies, C. (2008). Expecting success: Teacher beliefs and practices that enhance student outcomes. Verlog, Dr. Muller; Rubie-Davies, C. (2014). Becoming a high expectation teacher: Raising the bar. Routledge.

Notice that this tool includes instruction and assessment, as well as curriculum. Your responses can guide your efforts to address learning recovery and accelerate learning for all of your students. For example, there are several questions on grouping. We will focus on grouping more intentionally in Module 5 on instruction. There are also questions about assessment, which we will address in Module 6. And other questions on this tool allow you to reflect on the student goal setting that we discussed in Module 3.

 ## CASE IN POINT

Middle school history teacher Armando Cordova is known for the unit he developed on comparative religion. In the content standards, students are introduced to Buddhism, Islam, Judaism, Christianity, Confucianism, and Hinduism. Traditionally, these are taught based on a specific country (e.g., Medieval Japan includes Buddhism). But Mr. Cordova designed a unit that integrates each of these religions and provides students with historical context for each.

The lessons include note-taking guides and comparison charts so that students can keep track of the similarities and differences. Mr. Cordova has collected a number of videos that explain the core values and beliefs of each religion. In addition, his students had access to a variety of digital texts about these belief systems. There are also sections of the adopted textbook that contain information about each topic.

Sounds interesting—amazing, perhaps. But here's the thing. When Mr. Cordova reviewed the list of indicators of high expectations, he noted that he overdifferentiated in several areas. First, students were not all expected to read the content. As he said, "I think that there are lots of ways to learn, but I realize that some students didn't have to read anything to be successful in this unit."

Second, he realized that he did not have learning goals but rather focused on the tasks. As he said, "My students totally know what they need to do, but I doubt that they know what they are supposed to learn. That's on me. They deserve to know what they are learning from the tasks we are doing."

And finally, because students worked in groups to present to the class on a single religion, they did not need to know them all well. As he said, "By the end of the unit, some students knew Hinduism well but probably only a cursory amount of the others. I'm not sure that they could actually write a comparative religion paper, but the whole point is to be able to compare. This had made me think about my expectations and the experiences all of my students need to have to really understand this content well."

REFLECT

Take a look at the bulleted list of indicators for high expectations. Are there practices that you can change to ensure that students experience rigorous learning? Are any of Mr. Cordova's reflections resonating with you? Can holding high expectations for students help you support learning recovery?

CLARITY OF LEARNING

As noted in the information about expectations, teachers with high expectations communicate learning intentions and success criteria with the class. To do so, you have to know the grade level and content standards well. Some of the instructional materials we use have objectives included with them, but that does not mean that the teacher knows what students need to learn.

CAN HOLDING HIGH EXPECTATIONS FOR STUDENTS HELP YOU SUPPORT LEARNING RECOVERY?

Analyzing standards and developing an understanding of the concepts and skills embedded within those standards is an important part of teaching. It's the key to translating the official curriculum of the state, province, or country into classroom practice. This is where the curriculum really comes to bear on addressing learning recovery. An amazing lesson for fourth graders on second-grade standards is not going to ensure that students learn at high levels. Instead, those fifth graders are now ready for third-grade content.

There are a number of ways to analyze standards. A simple way is to take a look at the nouns (or noun phrases) and verbs (or verb phrases) in the standards. This provides clarity about the concepts (nouns) and skills (verbs) that students must master. This analysis can also help teachers understand the type of thinking required or the depth of knowledge needed to be successful. For example, some standards focus on one idea while others focus on several ideas. And still others focus on how ideas relate to one another or how ideas can be extended.

Let's take a look at an example from fifth grade:

Standard(s)	
Explain how an author uses reasons and evidence to support particular points in a text, identifying which reasons and evidence support which point(s).	
Concepts (nouns)	**Skills (verbs)**
Author	Explain how
Reasons	Support
Evidence	Identifying
Particular points in a text	

This simple analysis identifies the areas of content that students need to learn to be successful. As the teacher, you're on the lookout for students' understanding of these concepts and skills, which guides the development of instructional events and assessment opportunities.

Let's practice. Identify a standard or combination of standards that you will teach. Analyze the standard(s) for the required concepts and skills:

Standard(s)	
Concepts (nouns)	**Skills (verbs)**

As you probably noticed, the concepts (nouns) are fairly straightforward. But the skills (verbs) are a bit more complex. What does it mean to "explain how" when you are a fifth grader? How is that different from other grades that also use *explain*? In the English language arts standards, *explain* occurs at least forty different times. To maintain high expectations and a strong focus on learning recovery, we need to be clear on the skills students need to develop and the level of depth that is required by grade level. These make for great conversations with your colleagues.

Marzano and Simms (2013) identified the major cognitive moves that students must make to develop mastery of the standards (see Figure 5). This can help you and your team, but you still have to decide if you have high expectations for students in that particular grade level. Again, what does it mean to *explain* at the fifth-grade level? Turns out, that is a hard question to answer and one that plagues test-makers. It's an estimation, not an exact science. But to ensure that students' learning leaps rather than lags, it's important to focus on the skills (verbs) and the depth of knowledge implied by the standard as a whole.

Figure 5 Organization of Verbs in Standards

Add to: combine, deepen, improve, incorporate, integrate, introduce

Arrange: arrange, list, organize, sort

Big picture: comprehend, contextualize, orient, understand

Collaborate: collaborate, contribute, engage, interact, participate, share

Compare: associate, categorize, classify, compare, connect, contrast, differentiate, discriminate, distinguish, link, match, relate

Create: accomplish, achieve, build, compose, construct, create, develop, draft, form, generate, initiate, produce, publish, record, stimulate

Decide: choose, decide, select

Define: define, delineate, determine, discern, establish, exemplify, identify, interpret, label, locate, name, recall, recognize

Elaborate: broaden, derive, elaborate, enhance, expand

Evaluate: assess, check, critique, evaluate, judge

Execute: advance, calculate, conduct, compute, employ, execute, navigate

Explain: answer, articulate, clarify, communicate, convey, describe, explain, express, inform, narrate, present, recount, report, respond, retell, state, summarize, synthesize

Hypothesize: anticipate, approximate, conjecture, consider, estimate, experiment, explore, hypothesize, pose, predict, test

Infer: conclude, deduce, generalize, infer, reason

Measure: gauge, measure, quantify

Metacognitive: appreciate, attend, design, monitor, persevere, plan, prepare, reflect, self-correct

Problem solve: figure out, overcome, problem solve, resolve, solve, surmount

Prove/argue: argue, assert, challenge, claim, confirm, defend, disagree, justify, persuade, promote, prove, quantify, specify, support, verify

Pull apart: analyze, decompose, decontextualize, diagnose, examine, grapple, investigate, partition, probe

Redo: redo, repeat, reread, revisit

Reference: acknowledge, cite, consult, plagiarize, refer, reference, trace

Seek information: acquire, ask, capture, compile, detect, elicit, encounter, evoke, find out, gather, listen, note, notice, observe, question, request, research, search, seek, study

Symbolize: act out, chart, conceptualize, demonstrate, depict, diagram, graph, illustrate, imagine, map, model, represent, symbolize, visualize

Transform: accentuate, adapt, adjust, alter, apply, conform, convert, edit, emphasize, manipulate, modify, paraphrase, rearrange, refine, replace, revise, rewrite, shape, shift, simplify, strengthen, substitute, tailor, transform, translate, update

Source: Marzano, R., & Simms, J. (2013). *Vocabulary for the Common Core.* Marzano Research Lab (pp. 57–88).

Based on your analysis of the standards, you develop learning intentions success criteria. When students understand the learning goals, they learn more. The effect size is 0.51. It's worth the time and effort to ensure that students know what they are learning and how they will know what success looks like.

For convenience, we start learning intentions as follows:

I am learning . . . OR

We are learning . . .

And we start success criteria as follows:

I can . . . OR

We can . . .

EACH DAY, STUDENTS DESERVE TO KNOW WHAT THEY ARE LEARNING.

Of course, there are a number of other ways to ensure that students know what success looks like, including rubrics, exemplars, modeling, and so on. But for our purpose here, we'll focus on learning intentions and success criteria with these sentence starters. They'll get us all going on, making sure that students know what they are learning and what success looks like today. And today is important. Each day, students deserve to know what they are learning. After all, they are going to be judged based on whether or not they learned it. And students deserve to know what success looks like so that they can decide to allocate resources such as time and effort to accomplish the expectations.

There are a number of resources for developing learning intentions and success criteria (e.g., Almarode et al., 2021; Fisher et al., 2019), so we won't spend too much time here. Our point is that to accelerate learning, you have to know what students need to learn. The time invested in analyzing standards and identifying appropriate learning intentions and success criteria is worth it. Failure to analyze standards and design appropriate learning intentions and success criteria places students at further risk. Assistant Principal Christopher Martin has developed "The Proof of Learning Chart." This framework makes learning visible and transparent for his students. Figure 6 contains a one-day history class example.

Figure 6 Eighth-Grade History Example

Learning Intention: I am learning about how the Northern control of banks and business loans became a factor leading to the Civil War.	**Success Criteria:** • I can describe how Southerners felt when they were denied loans due to political and social views. • I can identify a list of economic assets for a typical Southern farmer in 1860 that could be seen as collateral for a bank loan. • I can justify why poor Southern farmers were denied loans from wealthy Northern banks due to a lack of viable collateral other than enslaved persons.
Written Expression: Write from the perspective of a disgruntled Southerner who cannot get a farming bank loan from a wealthy Northern bank. Explain why this is not fair and what you would like to see changed.	
Numeracy Connection: (FACT) Forty-eight percent of a Southern farmer's net worth in 1860 was from enslaved people. How would you provide the net worth of a typical Southern farmer in 1860? Use the identified list of Northern bank loan acceptable non-slave collateral in 1860 to calculate your answer.	**Assessments:** • Writing expression, short answer, or extended response reflection • Venn diagram on the North's and South's economic differences in 1860 • Other, something you and the teacher agree upon to show evidence of learning using the I can . . . success criteria
Social Learning Intention: Encourage classmates to express their views and ask questions during a debate or class discussion. Make others feel valued and welcomed by not interrupting when others share.	

Source: Christopher Martin, Hyre Learning Center, Akron, Ohio.

 CASE IN POINT

The second-grade teachers at Green Valley Elementary School met to analyze standards and identify learning intentions and success criteria. They found the process of naming the concepts and skills fairly easy, but it was much harder to agree on what the verb meant for their students. One of the standards that they focused on read, "Estimate lengths using units of inches, feet, centimeters, and meters."

As Brandi Weston said, "I'm not sure that I ever really paid attention to the word *estimate* like this. I mean, we teach them the measurement systems, but how close do their estimates need to be in order to be an estimate?"

Marco Jimenez agreed, adding, "I think we could see what they already know and how far off their estimates are. I think with some practice that they could get pretty good at this. But I don't have an answer to how close they need to be. I think we should make this part of the lessons when we focus on measuring, especially when they measure to determine how much longer one object is compared with another."

DO YOU KNOW WHAT YOUR STUDENTS NEED TO LEARN?

Ms. Weston responded, "Yes, that standard is clear to me. I think we can all agree on what it means to measure. And I agree with you that we could add the estimating into each lesson and some practice work we ask of students and their families so that we can see what we still need to teach them. Maybe we should include success criteria on this one in our lessons, like *I can explain my thinking when I estimate lengths*. This way, we can have them tell us what they were thinking so that we can figure out what they still need to learn."

As their conversation continued, they realized that they did not know what their students already knew. This pushes the conversation to the category of assessment but is an important consideration when it comes to the curriculum, as we will see in the next section.

REFLECT

How do you determine what your students need to learn? What considerations do you take into account when identifying the concepts and skills called for in the standards?

WHERE TO START THE CURRICULUM

As we noted earlier, this treads on the area of assessment. But the answer to this particular assessment question allows us to know where to start the curriculum. There is evidence that about 40 percent of instruction minutes are spent on things that students already know (Nuthall, 2007). Importantly, that 40 percent could differ from student to student. They all come to class knowing things. The problem is that some of them know this, and others know that, so we tend to teach everything that anyone might need to learn. Obviously, that's not very effective and will not allow us to accelerate learning to support learning recovery.

We need to know what students have already learned and what they still need to learn if we are going to allocate valuable instructional time and resources to recovery and acceleration. Of course, this also has implications for instruction and grouping of students, as we will see. But, for now, let's consider the curriculum (standards) as the starting place.

Imagine that you are teaching argument writing and you ask your students to write a short essay in which they argue a point and provide evidence. In doing so, you can identify which areas of the standard students already have mastered and where your lessons can contribute to students' progress. You will probably not be the last teacher to focus on argument writing with your students, as it is a skill that takes years to hone. But you can contribute to your students' skillset and ensure that they are on track with the expectations for their grade level. Some students may need help with the type of evidence they provide, others with making a claim. And still others may have difficulty stringing sentences along.

That's the nature of the work we do. But the question is, do we differentiate our curricular expectations for students based on their prior learning, or do we provide them access to complex and interesting tasks and shore up any skills that still need to be taught? In the past, there was a lot more differentiating that resulted in lowered expectations for some students. That has to change. We acknowledge where students are in their learning journey. They are where they are and it does no good to lament the fact that some did not learn. Instead, we use the knowledge about their current learning to accelerate and reboost their growth. Think of it this way: let's re-allocate the 40 percent of instructional minutes (on average) that focus on what a student has already learned and, instead, use those minutes to focus on what they need to know. Logical, right? And yes, in doing so, we can address any gaps in learning that we find. It's not the only solution, but it is an important one.

REFLECT

Consider the following questions as you develop an initial assessment to identify what students already know.

CONSIDERATIONS	YOUR RESPONSE
What do I already know about my students from previous units of instruction?	
What type(s) of assessment items will help me identify areas of prior learning? ☐ Writing sample ☐ Oral language or interview ☐ Knowledge inventory ☐ Other	How will I collect this information?
How can I ensure that my initial assessments are free from bias?	

PRIORITY CONTENT LEARNING

Over the years, there have been a number of conversations about key standards, essential standards, highly tested standards, and so on. We have not supported these efforts because students deserve to learn all of the standards expected of them. If not, equity gaps persist and can be exacerbated. And yet, we acknowledge that there are an awful lot of standards in some places for students to learn. The whole idea of narrow and deep doesn't seem to be in practice in a lot of standards.

Having said that, to recover learning, we have to ensure that students learn critical things that will impact their future. Yes, we want students to learn all of the standards, but in the short term, there are probably some standards that are a priority. In part, this can be addressed by recognizing that some students have already learned some things and don't need to be taught them again. And it highlights the idea that there are some standards that are gate-keepers. Perhaps, as we revisit standards in the future, we will actually reduce the breadth in favor of depth.

For the time being, it seems prudent to identify our nonnegotiable curriculum that all students need to learn and accelerate their learning on that. Of course, we teach the content that is outlined in the standards, but we concentrate on the curriculum that we believe is crucial for rebound. There are groups that are making recommendations about this, which can be useful in your discussions with colleagues. But you know your students, and we encourage you to use the recommendations and advice to make decisions.

FOR THE TIME BEING, IDENTIFY NONNEGOTIABLE CURRICULUM THAT ALL STUDENTS NEED TO LEARN AND ACCELERATE THEIR LEARNING ON THAT.

As Ainsworth (2013) has noted, the essential or priority standards are "a carefully selected subset of the total list of the grade-specific and course-specific standards within each content area that students must know and be able to do by the end of the school year in order to be prepared for the standards at the next grade level or course" (p. xv). Ainsworth compares these with supporting standards, which are standards that enhance the priority standards but do not receive the same amount of focused instruction and assessment. Priority standards should meet the following selection criteria:

- **Endurance** (lasting beyond one grade or course; concepts and skills needed in life). Will proficiency of this standard provide students with the knowledge and skills that will be of value beyond the present? For example, proficiency in reading informational texts and being able to write effectively for a variety of purposes will endure throughout a student's academic career and work life.

- **Leverage** (crossover application within the content area and to other content areas, i.e., interdisciplinary connections). For example, proficiency in creating and interpreting graphs, diagrams, and charts and then being able to make accurate inferences from them will help students in math, science, social studies, language arts, and other areas. The ability to write an analytical summary or a persuasive essay will similarly help students in any academic discipline.

- **Readiness for the next level of learning** (prerequisite concepts and skills students need to enter a new grade level or course of study). Will proficiency of this standard provide students with the essential knowledge and skills that are necessary for future success?

- **External exams.** The concepts and skills that students are most likely to encounter on annual standardized tests, college entrance exams, and occupational competency exams students will need to prepare for. (Ainsworth, 2013, pp. 25–27)

READINESS FOR THE NEXT LEVEL OF LEARNING IS CRITICAL SO THAT WE CAN RECOVER STUDENTS' LEARNING.

Interestingly, these criteria existed before the pandemics. At this point, it seems that readiness for the next level of learning is critical so that we can recover students' learning. Knowing where students are and the priorities for their learning allows us to focus on getting to the next normal and eventually raising the expectations for all students.

 CASE IN POINT

The first-grade team at Oak Drive Elementary were negotiating the priority curriculum for their students. As one of them said, "It's hard to decide. We've been teaching this for so long, it all seems important."

Jessie Manchester said, "I think we can agree that the foundational skills are critical. We have to work on phonemic awareness, phonics, and fluency. Those standards should be a major focus no matter what." The team quickly agreed.

Davis Baker added, "I think that there is a lot of writing that students do, and we could cut down some of the units and really focus on Standard 2. I think writing informational texts on a topic, with some facts, is really important. I agree that opinion is important and so are stories, but I propose we spend less time on those this year and really push the information. If that is really solid, I think it will serve them well."

Anne Mathis agreed and added, "I think one reading standard we can't do without is 5. They really need to learn the major differences between books that tell stories and those that give information. If they can do that, they'll understand a lot of future standards and we can integrate a lot of other ideas into that one standard."

As their conversation continued, the team agreed on a few standards that would ground their curriculum for the year. As Ms. Mathis noted, "I want to do more and I think we can actually teach a lot of standards this year, but I think it's really important to have this conversation and know which standards we think are the ones that are must-dos. If we can accomplish this, they're ready for second grade and we have time to address any needs that they didn't get last year. If we all do this, we can recover from this whole thing and maybe even be a little stronger."

REFLECT

What standards do you and your team need to focus on? What do your students need to learn now and what are you guaranteeing that all students will know and be able to do at the end of the year?

DESIGNING CHALLENGING TASKS

Students often speak of tasks (assignments) on a single continuum: easy to difficult. But this is only half the story when it comes to designing tasks. There's another continuum, which is cognitive complexity. Some tasks are more complex while others are less so. These two terms seem to be used interchangeably, but in fact, they are two different constructs. *Difficulty* is a measure of the amount of effort, time, or work needed, while *complexity* is a measure of the number of cognitive steps or potential outcomes (Webb, 1997). Some tasks require a lot of effort, such as washing a car. If you've never washed a car before, it is also complex because of the materials you need to assemble and use, decisions about the order to perform each of the steps, and so on. If you've done this lots of times, while the effort is still considerable, the complexity decreases because you have refined your car-washing procedures. The tasks we design for our students should be a balance of difficulty and complexity. We need for our students to (see Figure 7)

- increase their fluency (low difficulty/low complexity) such as applying past knowledge, using a familiar graphic organizer, or taking notes

- build their stamina (high difficulty/low complexity) such as independent reading or writing research papers

- exercise strategic thinking (low difficulty/high complexity) such as tasks that require metacognition, goal setting, or new learning tools

- encounter situations where they struggle (high difficulty/high complexity) such as project-based learning or close readings

Unfortunately, students not yet making expected progress are relegated to tasks below the line (fluency and stamina) with fewer opportunities to engage in strategic thinking and problem solving. The result is that learning is inhibited and students fail to make progress.

Figure 7   Complexity and Difficulty

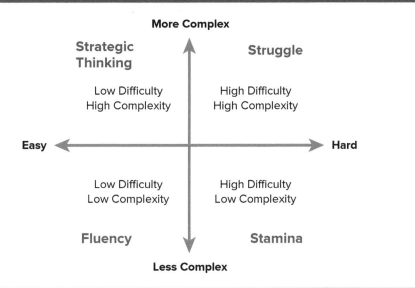

The design of a task sets students into motion. But getting the task just right can be tricky. If the task is too difficult or too complex, the learning may grind to a halt. But make the task too easy and it's "hands on but minds off." Students who regularly encounter tasks that require recall and reproduction, but little in the way of extended thinking needed for more complex tasks, lack the opportunity to learn grade-appropriate content. Don't get us wrong—we believe that fluency and stamina-building tasks are essential in learning design. But it's rare to encounter students who don't get enough of these low-complexity tasks. Quite the opposite—our experience has been that students with gaps or loss in learning don't encounter complex tasks very often.

So, you may be thinking, "But they can't do more complex tasks independently!" Keep in mind that more complex tasks often involve collaboration with peers and the teacher. Tasks that are in the struggle category typically involve some scaffolding from the teacher, such as doing a close reading and discussion of a challenging text. Strategic thinking tasks are often completed by heterogenous collaborative peer groups and involve goal setting, resolving problems, and reaching consensus. Consider some of your favorite tasks and examine how you might revise them in order to improve the complexity of tasks done during teacher-directed and collaborative small group learning (Mulhearn, 2018):

- **From closed to open:** How might this existing task be strengthened through creating multiple entry points and pathways, as well as multiple perspectives and solutions?

- **From information to understanding:** How might this existing task be improved by asking students to use many ways of knowing by applying critical thinking skills (compare and contrast; generalize; make connections and identify relationships)?

- **From telling to asking:** How might this task be more motivating by asking students to explore before explaining, leveraging student voice, using Socratic questioning, and fostering dialogue in the classroom community?

- **From procedure to problem solving:** How might this task foster interdependence and social cohesion by allowing students to identify the problem to solve, providing them insufficient information at first, giving them only some of the steps, or including some irrelevant information?

PAUSE & PONDER

Select a task you've been wanting to improve and recast it. What task did you select? In what ways did you revise it?

COMPONENT	BEFORE REVISION	AFTER REVISION
From closed to open		
From information to understanding		
From telling to asking		
From procedure to problem solving		

CASE IN POINT

Fourth-grade students in Ellery Jamison's class are studying the history of their state. This is a major part of the grade-level curriculum, and in the past, Mr. Jamison has formed small groups to conduct investigations about different topics. In previous years he differentiated tasks based on his perceptions of students' ability level and formed groups homogeneously. However, his grouping practices are now heterogeneous and he has been able to increase the complexity of each group's tasks. "It's helped me make sure that all the students, not just the ones who are on grade level, are getting exposed to more challenging content."

However, Mr. Jamison is encountering resistance from a grade-level colleague when it comes to redesigning this investigation. For many years, he and Karen Harrison have hosted a State History Fair for the school, with students in their classes profiling what they have learned with the third graders at the school. Although the big event is not taking place this year, the teachers still want the students to complete the investigation. Each student group gets a topic to investigate:

- Native peoples of the state

- Geographical and geological features

- Historical figures

- Economy of the state

- State and local government

In the past, the students have made group presentations, with varying levels of success. Mr. Jamison would like to revisit the tasks to increase the complexity, but Ms. Harrison wants to do the same thing they did last year. He was successful in convincing her to revise one task about Native peoples. He showed her how moving from a closed task to an open one would also address the social studies standard regarding evaluating events from multiple perspectives.

At this point, he has to decide if he is going to maintain the collaborative relationship with his colleague or go his own way and do what he believes is best for students and their learning. He talks with his principal, who says she will support him with his decision. He decides to make a list of pros and cons. What would you put on each? What would you decide based on the information you have?

SPRING FORWARD

There are several ways that we can, together, address learning recovery and accelerate students' achievement. In this module, we focused on the curriculum itself. Teachers must have high expectations of what their students can learn, and these expectations can be compromised when we focus on gaps and loss. When we analyze standards and develop learning intentions and success criteria aligned with rigorous expectations and knowledge of our students' prior learning, we can design instruction and intervention that makes a difference.

REFLECT

Reflect on your learning about recovering learning through curriculum. Identify actions you are considering based on your learning.

IMPORTANT

On a scale of 1 to 5, with 5 being very important and 1 being not important at all, how would you rate the value of recovering learning through curriculum in your classroom or school?

1   2   3   4   5

WAIT, BUT WHY?

Explain your reason for the rating above.

RECOVERING LEARNING THROUGH INSTRUCTION

In the last module, we focused on the curriculum and argued that educators needed to be clear about what students needed to learn. In doing so, they can partially address learning recovery. Once the areas of curriculum have been identified and educators know what students already know, deliberate instruction can move learning forward.

Creating meaningful learning experiences is a major way to accelerate what students know and can do. As we noted, a considerable amount of time (averaging 40% of instructional minutes) is spent on content students already know. In addition to the amount of time spent on content that has already been learned, there are instructional practices that simply do not work and further waste time. In fact, some of them could be considered educational malpractice. To address learning recovery and create learning leaps, instructional time must be used effectively. Simply said, we need to stop doing things that are ineffective and embrace the approaches that increase students' likelihood of learning.

But beyond that, students have developed significant skills with technology, and our future instructional moves should provide students regular and meaningful practice with the tools that do and will exist. It will serve us all well to keep our technology skills sharp. It may even help to future-proof our students and our profession.

WHAT YOU'LL LEARN

LEARNING INTENTIONS

- I am learning about quality core instruction that maintains learning growth.

- I am learning how to use instructional moves to accelerate learning.

SUCCESS CRITERIA

- I can identify instruction moves that ensure student learning.

- I can analyze the use of instructional minutes and maximize learning time.

- I can group students effectively for instruction.

- I can design appropriate practice tasks.

SELF-ASSESSMENT

Using the provided scale, identify your level of knowledge about addressing learning recovery through instruction. Consider each of these statements:

- I am aware of the components of effective instruction.

- I provide opportunities for my students to collaborate, interact with peers, and use academic language.

- I have plans for the instructional minutes in my class that maximize learning opportunities.

- I group students effectively for instruction.

(Continued)

(Continued)

- I design meaningful practice experiences that allow students to develop expertise.

IT STARTS WITH QUALITY-FIRST TEACHING

It almost goes without saying, but students need excellent instruction that results in learning. The meaningful experiences that teachers plan should deepen their understanding and allow them to recognize that they are learning. That did not change as a result of the pandemics. To recover learning, we need to do more. But if we don't first ensure that the instruction students experience is strong, then we face an uphill battle. In other words, if the core instructional experiences students have are not strong, then further ground will be lost as we collectively attempt to address student learning needs.

Thus, we start with the need for excellent learning experiences that are monitored for their impact. There are a number of excellent frameworks for instruction that have evidence that they result in better learning (e.g., Fisher & Frey, 2021). What does not work is a random collection of instructional strategies. Instead, students need coordinated, systematic, and purposeful experiences that move them from surface learning to deeper learning to eventual transfer and ownership of that learning.

One of the key features of strong instructional models is the value of collaboration or student-to-student interaction. When students have opportunities to talk with others, using academic language, they can learn a lot. In fact, classroom discussion has an effect size of 0.82, double the average impact on student learning. That's not to say that students should only be talking with one another in class. If you don't know anything about a particular topic, it's hard to have a meaningful conversation. But when you do have some ideas and you are able to discuss those ideas with others, noticing relationships and making connections, learning can accelerate. As Brown et al. (1989) noted, there are key features of a learning group:

- Collective problem solving
- Displaying multiple roles
- Confronting ineffective strategies and misconceptions
- Providing collaborative work skills

The reality is that a lot of classrooms are filled with teacher talk and very little student talk about learning. In many cases, distance and remote learning made that worse. In fact, there are many examples that suggest that students did very little talking with their peers or even with their teachers during distance learning. Regardless of what happened, the evidence is clear. We need to ensure that classrooms are filled with dialogue and not a monologue.

But there are optimal times for students to engage in peer-to-peer talking, in thinking aloud, and in dialogue with teachers and the whole class. When the focus is on the content, the "knowing that" and the subject matter vocabulary, then more teacher monologue or clear rubrics as to the content is desirable. But when they move to problem solving, deeper conceptual understanding, then there needs to be so much more student and student-to-student talk.

A reasonable goal is that, on average, 50 percent of the instructional minutes are spent in student-to-student interactions—this would mean ensuring that there was sufficient time and focus to the content-level instruction and appropriate time for the deeper relational instruction that leads to greater effective student talk. The other 50 percent is time that teachers are building or surfacing knowledge, or when students are engaged in independent practice. The 50 percent recommendation is not a hard-and-fast rule but rather something to aim for. Note that we did not say 50 percent consecutive minutes of student-to-student interaction. These interactions should be punctuated with think-alouds, practice, independent work, or questions. Later in this module, we'll have more on routines that save minutes and build students' ability to collaborate with their peers. For now, consider how much time students currently interact with their peers using academic language versus how much time they listen to you.

PAUSE & PONDER

Consider the experiences you believe your students have with peer interactions.

1. **My students listen to me talk for what percentage of the instructional minutes?**

| I spend little time talking (1%–25%). | I spend some time talking (26%–50%). | I spend a fair amount of time talking (51%–75%). | I spend most of the time talking (76%–100%). |

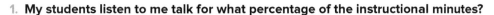

2. **My goal is for my students to talk with each other, using academic language for what percentage of the instructional minutes?**

| Very little (1%–15%) | Some (16%–30%) | A lot (31%–45%) | A balance (50%) |

3. **My plan for increasing student talk:**

As we have noted, there is more to instruction than student talk, but we wanted to start there because we believe it's not the specific strategies that are important. Instead, it is the decisions we make as students are learning, as we listen to them think aloud, as we give them alternate strategies and help them work with others to jointly advance learning, as we formatively evaluate our impact, that are important.

COGNITIVE APPRENTICESHIP

A cognitive apprenticeship model for teaching and learning suggests that there are additional instructional moves that teachers can take to deepen students' understanding (Collins et al., 1988). Spector (2016) outlined these moves to include the following:

STUDENTS NEED SYSTEMATIC AND PURPOSEFUL EXPERIENCES THAT MOVE THEM FROM SURFACE TO DEEP, TO TRANSFER OF LEARNING.

- **Modeling.** The teacher or expert models or demonstrates the desired knowledge and skill for the learner; this is typically necessary with new learners in a domain and can be repeated at various learning stages.

- **Coaching.** The teacher or expert observes a learner's performance and provides feedback aimed at helping the learning improve and become aware of specific aspects requiring improvement.

- **Scaffolding.** The designer or instructor deploys various support mechanisms for learners; these typically become less explicit and less supportive as learners gain competence and confidence.

- **Articulation.** The teacher encourages a student to talk about what he or she is doing or knows with regard to a particular task; this can occur at many points in an instructional sequence.

- **Reflection.** A teacher encourages a student to compare his or her response to a problem situation with that of an expert or possibly with that of another student as a way to draw attention to differences for purposes of developing understanding and insight.

- **Exploration.** A teacher provides students with opportunities to explore new problems and perhaps different types of problems requiring alternative problem-solving strategies. (p. 114)

PAUSE & PONDER

How do you provide students access to each of these learning opportunities?

Modeling	
Coaching	
Scaffolding	
Articulation	
Reflection	
Exploration	

Steven Kolari invited his principal to visit the class. Mr. Kolari is a veteran teacher who was known as effective but, as he said, "I know that there is more I can do to accelerate learning for my students. I want to be sure that I'm doing everything that I can." His principal, Angie Hise, asked what he was looking for in terms of feedback. Mr. Kolari responded, "I just want your eyes on the class again. What else can I do to make learning happen for my students?"

Ms. Hise observed a powerful lesson in which Mr. Kolari taught his students to compare numbers with a place value chart. Ms. Hise noted significant student engagement and Mr. Kolari's coaching and scaffolding.

When they met to talk about the lesson, Ms. Hise asked, "Where do you think you had your biggest impact in the lesson?"

Mr. Kolari responded, "I think that the scaffolding was pretty good. I don't think that I told them answers but gave them hints for them to do the real work. I coached and scaffolded a lot, but we got there, and they were able to use the place value chart successfully. I also think that their reflections at the end were really strong."

Ms. Hise, nodding, added, "Your scaffolds really seemed to move the learning. When Giselle was starting with the ones and getting confused, you asked her to think about the place value from left to right, like reading a book. She was almost instantly successful."

Mr. Kolari, after pausing for a few seconds, said, "But I didn't model. I never showed them my thinking when I noticed their patterns of errors. I ended up doing a lot more coaching and scaffolding because I think they were missing a mental model. Now that I think about it, I don't model that much in math, but I do all the time in reading and writing. That's the gap. That's what I need to do. Who models really well in math? I'd like to go see."

Ms. Hise answered, "Powerful reflections. Thanks for inviting me to be part of this. In terms of modeling, have you seen Melissa? She provides examples and thinks aloud but never gives them the answer. She's like you that way, but she does it more during modeling, and you do it more in scaffolding. I'm sure she would love to have you visit. I'm happy to cover your class so that you can spend some time with her. How about tomorrow or the next day?"

REFLECT

Who can you invite into your classroom or school to have this type of reflective conversation? What instructional strengths do you have, and what would you like to learn?

MAXIMIZING INSTRUCTIONAL MINUTES

Truth be told, there are a significant number of instructional minutes that are not used effectively. Students are often waiting for something to happen. The start of class is often filled with administrative details, which are necessary but do not impact learning. The end of lessons, before passing period or recess, is another time that can involve students packing backpacks or waiting to be released. There are transitions between activities. Sometimes instruction is paused as the teacher addresses problematic behavior. Further, a significant number of minutes are spent on providing instructions rather than instruction. Together, the estimate is that between 17 percent and 33 percent of instruction minutes are not used for learning (Fisher, 2009; Rathore, 2019). We're not saying that every minute can be used for instruction, as transitions are important and bathroom breaks are necessary. But what if we could increase the number of minutes focused on learning—academic, social, and emotional learning?

Williams (2018) suggests that increasing student achievement requires an increased rate of student learning, which in turn requires increased learning opportunities, which is predicated on increasing instructional time (see Figure 8). As we noted in Module 4, some students need more time, be that after the traditional school day or a longer school year. But we can accelerate learning by strategically using the instructional minutes that we have.

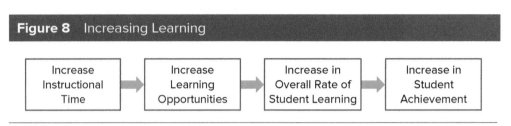

Figure 8   Increasing Learning

Source: Williams, C. (2018, September 19). *Minimizing lost instructional time.* https://www.csas.co/minimizing-lost-instructional-time

What would be different if we committed to starting class on time? How many more minutes of learning might we have? There are a number of tasks that teachers can apply to ensure that minutes are used well, even as they take attendance. For example,

- A fourth-grade class starts with a buddy-up conversation that integrates social and emotional learning.
- A high school science class starts with a writing prompt that activates background knowledge from a previous lesson.
- A kindergarten class engages in rhyming and chants to build phonemic awareness after recess and lunch as well as following each transition.
- A middle school math class starts with a "do now" challenge problem that students can work on individually or collaboratively. The problem draws on previous learning but is applied in a way that is not familiar to students.
- A high school English class starts with a poem of the day that students read and discuss with a partner. The poems are selected to elicit social and emotional learning opportunities and discussions.

There are a number of ways to start class that involve students' learning rather than waiting. In addition, there are strategies that teachers can use to engage students in meaningful thinking and learning through the end of the allotted time. Madeline Hunter (2004) coined the term "sponge activity" to describe "learning activities that soak up precious time that would otherwise be lost" (p. 117). She believed that sponge activities should (1) focus on a review of previously learned material and (2) provide distributed practice opportunities. Here are some examples:

- In their kindergarten class, when there are minutes before recess or lunch, the students practice number sense tasks that the teacher has ready for them at their tables.
- In their third-grade class, students create questions that they can use to stump the teacher or students at other tables. The key is that they must know the answer to their question and be able to explain it.

- In their middle school history class, the teacher keeps word sort tasks ready and provides students opportunities to sort words into categories. Then students explain the categories and how the words fit together to their peers.

- In their family and consumer sciences class, students compare recipes to predict which will have more protein, less sugar, or a balance of fats. This task requires that they apply their knowledge of ingredients to make these predictions.

Using instructional minutes well, from the start to the end, is important if we are going to recover students' learning and accelerate their performance. And we need to say this again, the use of these minutes is not limited to academics. As we have noted in several places in this playbook, it's important to recover the social and emotional aspects of learning as well. For instance, the few minutes at the end of the lesson can involve a self-assessment about their sense of agency that day.

In addition to the use of instructional minutes at the beginning and end of class, it's useful to consider how many minutes are spent providing students instructions about what they will do. Yes, students need clear instructions or they are likely to be off-task and asking for clarification. But how many minutes are spent providing instructions? If a middle or high school teacher spends ten minutes every fifty-minute period on instructions for 180 days, then thirty-six full class periods were spent on delivering directions. If an elementary teacher spends five minutes explaining what will happen during the day, ten minutes explaining what students will do in their centers or stations, and then another five minutes for various tasks during math, science, and social studies, the results are about forty-five minutes per day on instructions (or more), which equate to twenty-two days *each school year.*

What if we could reduce that by introducing some evergreen strategies? Are there some common routines that you can use that cut down the number of minutes spent on instructions so that you have more time for instruction? For example, in an elementary classroom, imagine that you have a word study center or a listening station or a writing response table. Once students know what is expected of them in each of those locations, the content can change but the task does not. And you will save a lot of time because you will not have to re-explain the directions each time students go to complete learning tasks.

There are also a number of collaborative routines that encourage student-to-student interaction and the use of academic language. But some teachers change these each week in an effort to "keep it fresh," and thus, students rarely get good at them. As we noted (Fisher & Frey, 2020), there are a number of processes that work. There is no one right way to teach. But consider the time savings if you select a few routines and build your students' habits. For example,

- **Collaborative posters.** In groups, students create a poster representing the main ideas of the concept. Students are given a rubric that describes what must be included in the poster. After thinking individually about how to represent their ideas, each student selects one color of pen and uses only that color on the chart. All students must contribute to both writing and drawing on the poster and signing it in their assigned color. Posters are displayed in the room so that students evaluate their own poster and at least one other using the rubric.

- **Reciprocal teaching.** Students work in groups of four with a common piece of text. Each member has a role: summarizer, questioner, clarifier, and predictor (Palincsar & Brown, 1986). These roles closely mirror the kinds of reading comprehension strategies necessary for understanding expository text. The reading is chunked into shorter passages so that the group can stop to discuss periodically.

- **Jigsaw.** Each student in the class has two memberships: a home group and an expert group. Each home group of four members meets to discuss the task and divide the work according to the teacher's directions. After each home group member has their task, they move to expert groups composed of members with the same task. The expert groups meet to read and discuss their portion of the assignment and practice how they will teach it when they return to their home groups. Students teach their expert portion to home group members and learn about the other sections of the reading. Finally, they return once more to their expert groups to discuss how their topic fits into the larger subject. This is an especially powerful instructional strategy, with an effect size of 1.20 (Hattie, n.d.; www.visible learningmetax.com).

- **Discussion roundtable.** Students fold a piece of paper into quadrants and record their thinking in the upper-left quadrant. This could be from a reading or video. They then take notes in other quadrants as students share their thinking. The final product is then a record of the viewpoints of each member of the group.

- **Text rendering.** Students read a piece of text, focusing on key points. When their group members have finished, each student shares a significant sentence. On the second round, each student shares a significant phrase, which does not need to be within the sentence they chose (and they record these). During the third round, each student shares a word from the reading that resonated with them (and they record these). The group then discusses the ideas generated.

- **Five-word summary.** Students read a piece of text and choose five words that summarize the reading. They then talk with a partner to reach consensus on five words that summarize the reading before joining another partnership. Now the four students reach agreements on the five words that represent the text. From there, they create their own summary of the text, using the five words agreed on by the group.

Note that these are easily adapted to blended learning and that students can use technology in the class or at home to complete these types of tasks. When done in a virtual space, students from different classrooms can work together. Of course, students need to be grouped effectively if these approaches are to work.

PAUSE & PONDER

Analyze your classroom schedule with the lens of increasing students' opportunities to learn. Consider both daily agendas as well as pacing guides.

Use the traffic light scale to consider each of the following:

- Time is flexible such that minutes can be allocated when larger numbers of students do not master content.

- There is a balance of reading, listening, speaking, and writing tasks across the day.

- In elementary classrooms, each subject area is allocated time.

- Class starts on time and minutes are used wisely.

- The schedule is clear such that students know what to expect.

Prioritize. Which of the above actions would you like to change? Highlight the one that you want to change and describe below what you will do to create that change:

GROUPING STUDENTS FOR ACCELERATION

As we noted in Module 4, teachers with high expectations use mixed-ability groups and re-group students often. This allows students to interact with a wide variety of peers and learn from a range of others. In practice, teachers group students in a variety of ways to deliver instruction and foster learning. The most common grouping practice by far is whole class instruction, in which all of the students are placed in a single group. However, exclusive whole class instruction is detrimental to learning at the elementary and secondary levels when compared to a healthy mixture of whole class, collaborative, and small group instruction. Group configurations can provide students with increased opportunities to learn and allow for acceleration of learning.

THE GROUPING DECISIONS UTILIZED BY THE TEACHER REFLECT THEIR EXPECTATIONS FOR STUDENTS.

There are two ways of grouping students for small group learning. The first is homogeneous grouping, in which students who share similar current performance levels are clustered. The second type is heterogeneous grouping, in which students who represent a range of knowledge and skills work together. Homogeneous small group learning should be reserved for some teacher-directed instruction. For instance, students with similar reading abilities work directly with the teacher in a lesson designed to address their specific needs. However, heterogeneous groups can be used for both teacher-directed and peer-led collaborative learning, in which students learn from one another. There are several advantages to heterogeneous grouping, whether teacher-guided or peer-led. These advantages include the use of peer resources within the group and increased participation levels by individuals, all within the presence of language and social models.

The ways students are grouped for teacher-directed instruction and peer-to-peer collaborative learning have an influence on what is learned (and not learned). In part, it is because the grouping decisions utilized by the teacher reflect their expectations for students. Researchers followed the mathematics progress of 3,000+ kindergarten English learners and compared them to the expectations of their teachers and their grouping practices. Their results linked the relative achievement of students to two factors: grouping and teacher expectations. Teachers with lower expectations for students relied more on whole group instruction and homogeneous small groups. Teachers with higher expectations used a combination of heterogeneous and homogeneous small group instruction and less whole group instruction. In addition, these teachers formatively assessed more often than those with lower expectations for students (Garrett & Hong, 2016).

Students who are not yet making expected progress are vulnerable to the grouping practices of teachers. Those who are in classrooms that use whole group instruction are less likely to receive ongoing formative assessments, and therefore less likely to have instruction adjusted to meet their needs. In addition, low-achieving students in peer-led homogeneous groups are more likely to languish because they lack the collective academic, language, and social resources necessary to progress. When it comes to students of concern, grouping can make a difference in students' learning.

Effective small group heterogeneous grouping is more than randomly assigning students to groups and hoping for the best. Student grouping should be intentional, assessment driven, and flexible. This is crucial for our students who are not yet making expected progress, as the ratio of higher- and lower-achieving students within the small group can play a factor. The needs of a single lower-achieving student in the presence of too many high-achieving ones can mean that one voice is drowned out as others dominate. Another consideration is the relative range within a group. A wide gap between the most accomplished and least accomplished students can pose a communication challenge that learners may not know how to bridge. In both cases, there is an increased likelihood that some students will dominate the task while others are left to passively observe.

STUDENT GROUPING SHOULD BE INTENTIONAL, ASSESSMENT DRIVEN, AND FLEXIBLE.

One method for constructing sound heterogeneous small groups is to use an alternate ranking system. Use a recent assessment formatively to rank students in order from highest to lowest achieving on this measure, then split the list in half to form two sublists. In a class of 32, Sublist A is students 1–16, while Sublist B is students 17–32. Use the top two from Sublist A and the top two from Sublist B to form a group of four students. Thus, Students 1, 2, 17, and 18 are a heterogeneous group. The next group comprises Students 3, 4, 19, and 20. The final group would be Students 15, 16, 31, and 32 (see Figure 9). Alternate ranking simultaneously accomplishes two purposes: maintaining heterogeneity across groups while also bracketing the relative range of cognitive, social, and language resources within. Of course, this isn't foolproof. Be sure to use your own knowledge of your students to make any necessary adjustments.

Figure 9   Alternate Ranking System Sample

1. Keisha	17. Rudolfo
2. Arturo	18. Sara

3.	19.
4.	20.
5.	21.
6.	22.

15. Leighanne	31. Felicia
16. John	32. Sam

Source: Frey, N., Hattie, J., & Fisher, D. (2018). Developing assessment-capable visible learners, grades K–12. Corwin.

PAUSE & PONDER

List students according to a recent assessment and use the alternate ranking system. As you examined the composition of each group, which factors did you consider in making any necessary adjustments?

Social strengths and needs	Interest or prior knowledge of topic
Gender	Primary language

CASE IN POINT

Eighth-grade science teacher Marc Lorimar has not made flexible grouping a part of his practice either prior to the pandemic or during distance learning. However, he has more recently been learning about grouping practices and has realized he needs to do more to address learning recovery and reach all of his students.

The science teacher decided to begin with his third-period class, as he felt that they were the most resilient across the day. "The instructional coach has always advised trying out new techniques in the class period that has a lot of comparative strengths," he said. He used the results from a practice test he had given the previous week. This no-stakes assessment isn't graded but gives him and his students an idea of how well prepared they are for next week's unit test. He rank-ordered his thirty-two students according to their practice test results to form in-class study groups, using an alternate ranking system. "It's just for two weeks, so I figured I could get a good sense of what's working and not working pretty quickly," he said.

For the next ten days, he had his students move into their study groups to conduct fifteen-minute review sessions. During that time, the teacher moved in and out of the groups, providing teacher-directed instruction as needed when study groups had difficulty with an assigned review topic. "My thinking was that I would give them a specific topic, like light energy behavior, so they could go back to the textbook and their lecture notes," he said. He did have a few incidents that were a problem. In one case, two of his students who had been dating each other had recently broken up but were assigned to the same study group. He ended up moving another student, who is an English learner, to a group that had another student who shared her heritage language. Then there was the case of one group of particularly rambunctious students. "I ended up moving a few students to other groups," he chuckled.

The results of the assessment were of interest to Mr. Lorimar. "I wanted to see how the kids did and whether I could detect any movement compared to previous tests," he said. He noticed that several of his lowest-performing students earned scores that were the best they had yet achieved. "I'm a runner, and it was great to talk with each of them about their PR—their personal record," said the teacher. He also said that two students who he has been concerned about did not perform as well as expected. "I've got some more work to do," he said.

REFLECT

According to this scenario, what did you see as being positive actions? What advice would you give for next steps? Was there anything problematic?

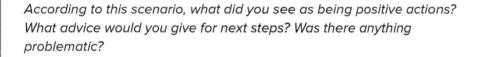

THE CASE FOR PRACTICE

This module has focused on instruction, but it's only part of the equation. Students need to engage in meaningful practice in order for the instruction (and learning) to stick. The challenge is to ensure that students actually practice. Why is it that a student will spend hours practicing a sport but not algebra? Why will a student practice the drums daily but not reading? In part, we believe that this is due to the lack of a mental model of expertise. The student who engages in hours of sports practice likely has an idea about what really good playing looks like. And the student who engages in hours of drum practice probably knows what it sounds like to be a strong drummer. Can we say the same about academics?

The research on deliberate practice, which has an effect size of 0.79, is helpful in thinking about the types of practice students should do. And note the term "deliberate," as it is not practice, practice, practice—indeed, some students can practice the wrong strategies, some cannot and do not seek feedback to improve the focus of their practice, and some have little understanding of what success looks like, so they struggle to use practice to improve. The Deans for Impact (2016) developed the following visual based on Andres Ericsson's research on deliberate practice (Ericsson et al., 1993).

The Five Principles of Deliberate Practice

PUSH BEYOND one's comfort zone

Work toward well-defined, **SPECIFIC GOALS**

FOCUS intently on practice activities

Receive and respond to **HIGH-QUALITY FEEDBACK**

Develop a **MENTAL MODEL** of expertise

Source: Deans for Impact. (2016). *Practice with purpose: The emerging science of teacher expertise.* Austin, TX: Deans for Impact.

According to this model, when students have a mental model of expertise (which is aided by students' understanding of the success criteria), they are more likely to receive and respond to feedback. And they are more likely to focus on the practice activities as they work toward a goal and push themselves as they struggle. Note how many of these aspects of deliberate practice we have already addressed in this playbook. For example, we talked about the value of struggle and the importance of goals. Together, the five principles of deliberate practice can accelerate learning. The fact is that they're not always present, and thus the results are not realized. Addressing learning recovery requires that we mobilize all of the information we have and actually put it into practice.

What is practiced and how it is practiced matters. Rote repetition will not result in improvement. Deliberate practice requires attention on the part of the learner.

That's in part what makes it deliberate. Part of the instructional time allotted in the classroom should be dedicated to deliberate practice. We don't mean mindless worksheets completed silently by students. Rather, effective teachers create conditions for practice that takes place in classrooms by (Brabeck et al., 2010):

- Modeling problem-solving processes

- Designing partially completed examples on which students can practice

- Sequencing activities logically

- Spacing practice activities appropriately

- Monitoring student practice providing guidance and feedback

One area of the curriculum that is likely to require a more significant investment is writing. Students need to write more and receive feedback about their writing (Frey & Fisher, 2013), which has been especially difficult during COVID teaching (Webber, 2020). In terms of practice, it's about the investment students need to make in planning, drafting, and revising their writing. And it's about seeking feedback about the impact that their writing has on others. There are a number of ways that we can leverage what we have learned from COVID teaching to provide students an opportunity to practice and receive feedback about their writing (see Figure 10).

WHAT IS PRACTICED AND HOW IT IS PRACTICED MATTERS.

Figure 10   Options for Writing Practice and Feedback

Key Idea	Description
Live writing in individual shared documents or digital notebooks	Each student has a document they write online that the teacher can also see and comment on. They respond to tasks in the document. The document can be blank or set up with images, links, and structured guidance (e.g., Google Docs, OneNote—stand-alone or built into Google Classroom/Teams).
Live writing in group documents with individual pages or areas	Similar to the above but each student is essentially writing into the same document for the whole class (i.e., a section in a document with their name on it); everyone can see other students' writing, or they can work collaboratively. The teacher can see each student's contributions in their sections.
Using slides as a writing space	As above but using Google Slides for writing—each slide pre-prepared with textboxes, and students write on their own page. Easy to see each students' writing and scan between them during the lesson. Easy to link to tasks and resources, to create templates.
Using forms for short answers	Use forms in Google or Teams to set multiple questions. Students respond to questions individually, and the teacher exports them into a spreadsheet to see answers from each student. A helpful tip is to make Q1 the student name for easy identification. Answers can be long or short—good for seeing lots of answers side by side to the same questions.

(Continued)

(Continued)

Key Idea	Description
Using shared spreadsheets	As before, but going straight into the spreadsheet—students write short answers into their allocated column (harder to mask students' answers from each other).
Digital whiteboards	Lots of apps/platforms offer this popular feature. Students write on their digital board and then share their responses as requested. The teacher sees them on screen all at once—answers can be long or short; feedback is given verbally or written to individuals or class depending on the platform (e.g., whiteboard.fi). Students and teachers can also write over PDFs of documents.
Digital sketch pads	Similar to whiteboards, but students have their own space on a bulletin board that is easy for the teacher to see all at once—or scrolling through. See writing progress in real time and add comments for the whole group or individuals as they work.
Voice/audio notes	Using voice recording add-ons to record verbal feedback—much quicker to record than to write the same amount. Students can playback live or later if done asynchronously.
Photographs of work	The basic idea of taking pictures of handwritten work or other nonelectronic work and then uploading them to share with the teacher. Various dedicated apps and use of phones as scanners. Teachers can annotate and return or use for verbal feedback.
Using platform chat function	Making use of chat function in Google Meets, Teams, Zoom—to see students' answers to questions. Good for spontaneous dynamic responses in addition to verbal responses in live sessions. A good tip is to use a whiteboard-style countdown so students submit answers simultaneously—so they can't just copy answers given.
Standard email	Simply sending work back and forth via email—straightforward for longer pieces such as essays or chunks of work completed offline—not for live lessons.
Question response add-ons	Platforms that allow questions to be set in a dynamic way during live lessons or planned in advance, e.g., multiple-choice or written answers—good for diagnostic questions. Various apps track each student's response—as well as creating poll graphs, word cloud responses, etc.
Verbal feedback in live session	The obvious thing of selecting only certain students or small groups to be on camera at any point to discuss work directly—work perhaps shared via emailed photographs or live document sharing.

Source: Sherrington, T. (2021). Remote learning solutions: Crowd-sourced ideas for checking students' writing. *Teacherhead.* https://teacherhead.com/2021/01/10/remote-learning-solutions-crowd-sourced-ideas-for-checking-students-writing

Importantly, the practice we're talking about is not simply homework. Assigning more homework will not address students' learning recovery needs. A significant amount of homework is assigned because the teacher ran out of class time (MetLife, 2008). When homework is assigned to provide opportunities for deliberate practice of some curricula already taught, then it can have more impact. As we noted earlier, it's important to use class time well. And, as we noted in Module 4 on curriculum, it's valuable to know what students need to learn and then align instructional minutes to ensuring students are successful. Homework is not effective for younger students up to third grade; for older students, it is of value, provided it is properly constructed (Campitelli & Gobet, 2011).

It is the suitability of the practice for the learner that matters. Whether they are practicing a single skill that they are learning or a mixture of previously mastered and newly learned skills (cumulative), the learner's competence matters. Whether in class or out of class (homework), the learner should be taught to an initial acquisition level of at least 85 percent success (Hughes & Lee, 2019). By ensuring that learners have attained a high rate of accuracy during instruction, the practice they engage in is more likely to be done correctly. There is little benefit to practicing something incorrectly without feedback. In the case of homework, we are looking for productive success. Figure 11, developed by Reading Rockets, a national multimedia project of research-based literacy strategies, provides a summary about homework practice that has the potential to accelerate learning.

ASSIGNING MORE HOMEWORK WILL NOT ADDRESS STUDENTS' LEARNING RECOVERY NEEDS.

Figure 11 More Effective Homework Practices

Practice	Explanation
Give less more often.	Distributed practice is critical for maintenance and retention. Providing multiple, smaller practice opportunities is superior to a single, large practice session.
Have a specific purpose in mind for each student.	Have a specific goal for the student to accomplish and understand the value of the assignment for each student.
Ensure the task mirrors the instruction.	For example, if instruction has been limited to the knowledge level, requiring students to use the content for application in a new format is not appropriate.
Allot enough time to present homework and ensure student attention.	Because many students write slowly and have difficulty with multiple step directions given orally, rushing through the presentation of homework may mean students will not know what to do. Make sure students are listening when you are giving an assignment.
Verify student understanding of the assignment.	Merely asking students if they understand the assignment does not verify that they do. If the task is new and unfamiliar, it may be helpful to demonstrate how it is done.
Explain the purpose of the homework and how it will be evaluated.	Explaining why the homework is important and what it is designed to do may help students be more motivated to complete it. Standards for grading should be made explicit to students and their understanding ensured.
Provide feedback in a timely fashion.	Homework should be evaluated as soon as possible and written or oral corrective feedback given to students. This is especially important if students have not yet mastered the targeted content or skills.

Source: Ruhl, K., & Hughes, C. (2010). Effective practices for homework. *Reading Rockets.* https://www.readingrockets.org/article/effective-practices-homework

SPRING FORWARD

Designing powerful instructional experiences for students is a necessary part of the teaching and learning process. The practices we use should have evidence that they will impact learning, and we should change them if they do not impact learning. We need to use the time we have wisely, build students' learning habits, and structure learning groups for success.

REFLECT

Reflect on your learning about instruction and the ways in which instructional decisions impact students' learning and your ability to address learning recovery. Identify actions you are considering based on your learning.

IMPORTANT

On a scale of 1 to 5, with 5 being very important and 1 being not important at all, how would you rate the value of focusing on instruction to address potential learning loss and accelerate learning?

1   **2**   **3**   **4**   **5**

WAIT, BUT WHY?

Explain your reason for the rating above.

MODULE 6

RECOVERING LEARNING THROUGH ASSESSMENT

Assessment provides information that teachers can use to make decisions. At the most obvious level, teachers use assessment information to determine if there are gaps in student learning. Teachers can also use assessment information to identify what students already know so that valuable time is not spent on content students have already learned.

Further, assessment information can be used to determine when students have learned something so that the focus of instruction can progress. And assessment information can be used to make adjustments to the lessons and tasks if students are not making progress.

In fact, assessment is one of the keys to accelerating learning and learning recovery. We need to know if there are gaps in student learning, and if so, on what skills and concepts. And we need to know if the lessons we design are effective in addressing the needs or if we need to add interventions. Without this type of information, we run the risk of teaching the same things that we always did, assuming that they all need it and will all learn it. We can learn to be much more precise for the students that are in front of us now as well as those who need us in the future.

WHAT YOU'LL LEARN

LEARNING INTENTIONS

- I am learning about the impact of deficit thinking as a barrier to student progress.

- I am learning about how to curb assessment bias.

- I am learning about the relationship between initial and confirmative assessments.

- I am learning about how to apply flexible assessment tools.

- I am learning about how to gauge my impact to make decisions about acceleration.

SUCCESS CRITERIA

- I can take an inventory of my assessment tools.

- I can measure my impact on students' learning by measuring effect size.

SELF-ASSESSMENT

Using the provided scale, identify your level of knowledge about assessment to aid in learning leaps. Consider each of these statements:

- I am knowledgeable about types of bias in judgments about assessment data.

- I utilize universal response as part of my assessments.

- I utilize teach-back as part of my assessments.

(Continued)

(Continued)

- I utilize writing as part of my assessments.

- I co-construct rubrics with my students to deepen their learning.

- I conduct a process for measuring my impact on student learning.

INFORMATION IS NECESSARY

To address learning recovery and focus on acceleration, teachers need to know what students already know, what they need to know, and how they are progressing from what they know to what they need to know. In other words, we teach to reduce the gap between what students already know and what they still need to learn. That did not change when we changed the medium of teaching. What might have changed is some students' current level of understanding and performance; what might have changed is some students' understanding of their progress toward the success criteria. And what should change is the increase in the use of frequent, low-stakes assessments that allow teachers to make good instructional decisions and students to know their progress.

In order to understand students' learning recovery needs and begin the process of acceleration, we need to begin with back-to-school assessments. Regardless of whether you return to in-person learning at the start of the school year or sometime after the year begins, it is crucial to see where students really are in their learning. The practice of back-to-school assessments is arguably more common in the primary grades. However, we can't afford to wait weeks until the first exam is completed to begin to learn where the gaps are. The risk in saying that is that we might bore or scare students if we say, "Welcome to school. Here's your test." We believe that we can be more subtle than that. For example, a middle school English teacher typically engages her students in a range of team-building activities during the first week of school. As she says, "I want to build trust so I start slow and focus on relationships. Then, when we have a strong climate, I can go fast."

This year, she added a written reflection to some of the team-building tasks. For example, students were asked to create a structure that would allow four people inside and they had limited supplies. Once finished, they were asked to write about the ways in which their team communicated and solved the problem. As the teacher said, "I wanted to see where their writing was so I would know where to start with whole class and small group instruction. Rather than start the class with the unit on argument writing like I usually do, I wanted to identify areas of need for my students."

There are a wide variety of back-to-school assessments that teachers can use. Of course, there are more formal assessments that can be used to identify needs. For example, iReady and MAPs can be used to identify areas of need, as can LevelSet by Achieve3000. There are a lot of tools that school systems can use to help teachers know what students still need to learn. In districts where benchmark assessments are used, one should be administered in the first two weeks of school so that teachers can get an early sense of what needs to be taught and to whom. In addition, teachers can adapt, adopt, or develop assessments that they can use. Before we explore some examples of these assessments, it's important to recognize that the information gained from these tools is valuable in planning instruction but can result in deficit thinking. As we noted earlier in this playbook, lowered expectations for students are not going to help them recover learning. Knowing where they are and doing something about it will help.

LOWERED EXPECTATIONS FOR STUDENTS ARE NOT GOING TO HELP THEM RECOVER LEARNING.

DEFICIT THINKING VERSUS REASSEMBLING LEARNING

Assessment information can be a double-edged sword if we are not careful. There is a risk in exploring where students are now in their learning journey. That risk is in engaging in deficit thinking. When teachers examine data about what students cannot currently do, they run the risk of thinking that those students will never be able to do it. Or they end up with low expectations for students in the belief that a little growth is good enough. As Valencia (2012) noted, "Deficit thinking blames the victim for school failure, instead of examining structural factors, such as segregation and inequities in school financing, that prevent low-SES students of color from achieving" (p. 611). Importantly, it's not just students who live in poverty or those who are from traditionally underrepresented groups that can be victims of deficit thinking. In a time when there is much speculation about learning loss, all current students are at risk of the deficit thinking that results when there is discussion in the popular press about a "lost generation" due to COVID-19 (Meckler & Natanson, 2020). We appreciate what the former executive director of the American Mathematical Society says about viewing learning loss differently:

> Mathematicians know that stepping away from a topic for a while requires time to recollect the bits and pieces when you return. Those bits and pieces aren't lost—they only require reassembling, and often the reassembling leads to greater understanding. (Ewing, 2020)

The challenge is that many of our students have experienced traumas and are struggling just to make it to school. But feeling sorry for them and lowering our expectations for their learning will not help. As we noted in Module 4, there needs to be a range of supports that help students address the experiences that they have had. And they need their teachers to create meaningful learning experiences that focus on acceleration. Will we recover all of the learning all of our students need to do in one year or two years? We don't know. But if we don't expect them to learn and achieve, they probably won't.

Let's shift our language to talk instead about reassembling learning. The starting point when reassembling anything is figuring out what pieces you have. Assessment can tell us what pieces we have and what's missing. When you review the data that reflects your students' current level of performance, refuse to accept that the data are fixed or that the data reflect the personal characteristics of the student. Remember, we are all on a learning journey, and there is no bad place to be. Our role is to ensure that students have every opportunity to experience greatness.

WATCH OUT FOR BIAS IN ASSESSMENT

All of us like to think that we are completely rational thinkers when it comes to assessment. After all, we design the assessment, the students take it, and we grade it. It's all there in the utterly logical results derived from their performance. However, the fact is that we are hardwired to be pattern-seekers who look for cognitive shortcuts to help us quickly form conclusions (Tversky & Kahneman, 1974). These cognitive shortcuts are not necessarily bad ones. You look at a street with lots of traffic on it and rapidly make some decisions that will help you safely cross it. But those cognitive shortcuts can do a disservice to students when it comes to assessment. These biases may be heightened because we are unsure of what to expect in terms of student assessment results. Laura Greenstein (2019), founder of the Assessment Network, cautions that a number of specific biases color the way we design and interpret assessment results, thus serving as a barrier of our own construction.

- **Confirmation bias.** The search for further evidence to confirm what we already believe to be true. Viewing some assessment data that confirm there are many gaps in learning, while disregarding other data that point to gains, is an example of confirmation bias.

- **Optimism bias.** When we dismiss a student's learning gap because we want to believe they are doing just fine. After all, if the students are doing well, then the teacher is too, right?

- **Pessimism bias.** "See, I told you everything was awful! These children are never going to learn to read because they don't know all their letter sounds!" Call this the Chicken Little Effect—the sky is falling and there isn't anything we can do about it.

- **Reliance on partial information.** We're all guilty of this at times. We think we know the whole story, and therefore we stop seeking out more information. For instance, a student's trauma is used as the reason why they aren't making progress in math, without investigating what academic gaps may exist.

- **Illusion of knowledge.** This is the belief that we know more than we actually do. This leads to overconfidence in one's own decision making, compared to the judgments of others who are less familiar to us and therefore are not regarded. "Never mind what the new district assessment coordinator says about the reading benchmark. I've taught fourth grade for ten years and I know what this means."

- **Status quo bias.** Perhaps the greatest danger in the face of unprecedented changes in education: the desire to simply go back to doing the things we always did for assessment because that's what we're familiar with. Status quo bias has been an important inspiration for *Rebound*.

It's important to know that we are most vulnerable to committing bias errors when we are feeling under a great deal of pressure, are anxious, and feel stressed. Let's accept that we are not Mr. Spock in *Star Trek*, always making logical decisions. Emotion plays a role in what we do and in how we decide what assessment data reveal. So let's take a page from the Visible Learning database to reduce bias in assessment:

- Be clear on the success criteria for students from the beginning of each unit.

- Involve students in the direct monitoring of their learning progress so that you are not the only one doing so. Learning accelerates when the student, not the teacher, is taught to be in control of learning.

- Make feedback part of a high-trust environment that is fully integrated into the learning cycle (not just at the end of the cycle).

- Use a range of assessment and instruction approaches so that students can demonstrate their mastery in more than one way.

- Know how to gauge your own impact on learning by using initial and confirmative assessments in tandem.

CASE IN POINT

Marco Ruiz is at his desk looking at data. Across from him sits his teaching partner Dania Herrera. Mr. Ruiz says, "I expected much, much worse. I'm not sure why. Maybe it's the news. They talked about all of the students not learning. But these initial assessments are not that bad. I've seen worse and I've seen better. I am worried about a few of our kiddos, like Lissette here. She is way behind. Do you have her information from last year?"

Ms. Herrera digs through the pile and finds it. "Oh, she was absent a lot. And the year before, she had almost perfect attendance. Something must have happened. We need to pay close attention to her and make sure she's at school every day and getting some extra love. We've got a new attendance plan in place, and Lissette should definitely be on their radar. I'll circle back to them to make sure she is and find out what we need to do with the early warning team."

"What about Leo? The back-to-school assessment that we did shows that he is really low. What was he like in the past?"

Ms. Herrera responds, "I can't really tell. There isn't a lot of information about him. I see that he was here three years ago, but then he went to a different school two years ago. And last year, he seems to have disappeared. I'm not sure what we need to do for him."

Mr. Ruiz nods. "Maybe we could get him some tutoring? Or maybe he could start the after-school specialized program? Could you call his mom and try to talk with her about some options? I think we need to know more and create a whole system to get him learning again."

Ms. Herrera interjects, "Sorry to interrupt, but did you see these four? Look at them! They made fantastic progress. They were a bit behind the year before and now are fully at grade level. We need to get them teaching others and we're going to need to think about how to keep them accelerating."

Their conversation continues as they note students in need and how to support their learning. Overall, they noted that about 20 percent of the students in their classes were really struggling. As Mr. Ruiz says, "I'm trying not to get overwhelmed. We have a lot going on and I think the changes we've made will really help. It's just going to be really important not to give up on our students. They need us more than ever."

INITIAL ASSESSMENTS DETERMINE WHERE THEY ARE

Assessments at the outset of the year or a new unit of learning help teachers identify student needs and reduce the amount of time spent on content that has already been learned. This recoupment of instructional time is a key to acceleration. Initial assessments do not need to be particularly long or elaborate. We'll provide a few examples that teachers have used but know that there are a lot more possibilities.

- Kindergarten and first-grade teachers collaborated to develop a readiness inventory that included numbers, letters, sight words, colors, and so on. As one of them said, "A lot of our students didn't attend kinder this year, so we need to see where they all are. We completed the inventory the first week of in-person school as we played games, so it didn't really feel like a test."

- Third-grade teachers used a writing inventory to review students' performance from the previous year. They collected writing samples each month to monitor progress and make adjustments in the learning intentions for students. As one of them said, "I like the idea of continuing to monitor the same set of skills and setting the expectation that all of our students will get there if we keep focused."

- Middle school math teachers adapted an algebra readiness assessment that they had used in the past to determine which students would take the class in eighth grade. As one of them said, "We stopped using this assessment for readiness a couple of years ago, but I think it will help us figure out where they are and identify things that students need to learn."

- High school science teachers used a vocabulary assessment to determine students' understanding of key technical terms. As one of them said, "If they know the term, they know something about the concept. This will help us know which of the major concepts we need to re-teach to make sure our students are successful."

We could go on as there are a number of different tools that teachers can use. Our point is that teachers need to know what their students have already learned and what they still need to learn at the start of the year and at the beginning of each major unit of instruction.

PAUSE & PONDER

Take inventory of your assessment tools. Use these questions to guide your process.

QUESTIONS	NOTES AND REFLECTIONS
What assessments of prior student learning do I currently have access to?	
How can I gather information to determine what students already know?	
How can I collect information on student strengths to build upon?	
How can I collect information to determine what areas of learning need improvement?	
What strengths do I have in regard to data collection and analysis?	

QUESTIONS	NOTES AND REFLECTIONS
What opportunities do I have in data collection and analysis?	
What additional information do I need to determine current student performance levels?	

 CASE IN POINT

As we have noted, initial assessments are not limited to the beginning of the school year. The sixth-grade teachers at Johnson K–8 Academy were several units into the school year and about to begin a series of lessons about explanatory writing. As one of them said, "Our standards introduce argument writing in this grade so they wouldn't really have missed anything last year. In fifth grade, they focused on opinion writing, so the first couple of units were all new to everyone. We focused on things like organization and voice as needed, but they all needed to learn about argumentation. But this set of lessons focuses on informative writing and they really didn't get this information last year. So, we're expecting some gaps and we've added some extra support for students."

When the school was engaged in distance learning, the teachers began to record interactive videos and added them to their learning management system. These videos introduced students to various aspects of informative writing and could be assigned, as needed, to students. The videos had integrated quiz features that allowed the teachers to monitor students' progress. One teacher explained, "This is a practice that worked really well in distance learning. We knew we wanted to keep this going on the return to school. We each developed a few videos and then we shared them with the team so students could see them all. This added practice and more time that we didn't have in the classroom. It's now part of the blended learning that we want to keep going at school."

One of the things that these teachers noted was that different students had different needs. This is an important realization when we discuss the idea that about 40 percent of the content has already been learned. That 40 percent could differ from student to student. For example, some students struggled with appropriate introductions for informational writing. Others added their opinions. And still others failed to cite sources. A number of students had run-on or fragmented sentences. Another teacher said, "They each have some strengths based on what they learned in the past, and a unique set of learning needs. Our job is to know what those are and create lessons that are appropriate for them. The technology helps us but so does the small group time. We have a common expectation for our students and we're doing everything that we can to get them there. The interactive videos allow us to monitor progress and address some of the needs at the same time."

Another teacher added, "If we didn't have the technology, I'm not sure that we would be able to catch them all up. In fact, we had to create even more resources for practice once we had the initial assessment information. But, honestly, it's been really rewarding to see the progress and know that we're meeting a need."

REFLECT

Do you sense teacher agency in this example? What role did the initial assessment play? How are these teachers making adjustments to ensure their students learn?

FLEXIBLE ASSESSMENT TOOLS

Initial assessments are not the only ones teachers use. We also use other assessment tools in flexible ways to monitor students' progress along their learning journey. Sometimes, we use the information gained to make instructional decisions, and other times to provide students and their families with a reflection of their learning. These tools are not inherently formative or summative. Rather, it is the purpose for the use of the tool that matters. Not unlike the tools on your hardware bench, most assessment tools can be used for a variety of purposes. And like your hardware tools, it is a matter of choosing the right tools for the job.

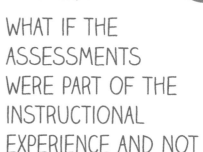

To accelerate learning, we need more frequent assessment, not less. That seems counterintuitive as assessments are historically perceived as taking time away from instruction. But what if the assessments were part of the instructional experience and not a separate event? What if they were used to inform teachers and students what they already know, how far or close they are to the success criteria, and where they should move next?

WHAT IF THE ASSESSMENTS WERE PART OF THE INSTRUCTIONAL EXPERIENCE AND NOT A SEPARATE EVENT?

MODULE 6

Assessment through universal response. Universal response opportunities are one example of simple informal assessment. The idea has been around a long time but isn't always used, especially outside of the primary grades. The idea is that students are provided an opportunity to respond simultaneously to a question or task. This encourages participation and allows the teacher to see thinking and make adjustments in the lesson in real time. Universal response systems prompt stronger teaching practices, too, as teachers give more feedback in these circumstances (Haydon et al., 2013).

Response cards that have *Agree* and *Disagree* written on them are an example. Personal whiteboards are also an option. Hand signals are another. Chat blasts and reaction buttons are an option. Polling systems are yet another. In fact, one of the things many of us have discovered during distance learning is that the use of frequent low-stakes polling questions has increased engagement and participation.

There are lots of ways to elicit a simultaneous response from students. During distance learning, we set a goal to provide students a universal response opportunity at least every ten minutes. Originally, this was to encourage participation and engagement as some students had their cameras off or did not respond in the chat. But the impact was greater than that. These universal response opportunities provided teachers with information about their lessons. Were they going too slowly? Was something not clear? Were some students successful while others needed additional instruction?

If we really want to accelerate and reassemble their learning, students need opportunities to engage and participate. Teachers need regular feedback from students about their success. We should end the practice of calling on one student at a time to answer or respond and instead provide regular, planned opportunities for all students to respond. And we should commit to using the information we gain from these universal responses to make decisions that allow us to accelerate learning.

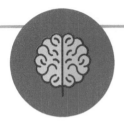

DRAW ON YOUR EXPERTISE

How many of these universal response systems can you use in your classroom to increase assessment and feedback opportunities?

	YES	NO		YES	NO
Hand signals			Whiteboards (digital or physical)		
Response cards			Polls		
Line ups			Collaborative response boards (e.g., Padlet)		
Chat blasts (all respond at once)			Reaction buttons		

CASE IN POINT

Jesse Piña uses personal whiteboards as one of the universal response opportunities with his fourth graders. As he said, "I didn't use these before, but I saw a colleague using them during distance learning and I saw a whole level of engagement and how the teacher could scaffold better based on the information she got from the students' work. I kept this up as we returned to the building, and it really helps me monitor my students and make adjustments to the class."

For example, Mr. Piña noted that his students' spelling wasn't strong, so he decided to have daily spelling tests. But students use their personal whiteboards to write the words and then show him. He then reads the word, saying all of the letters, and students mark directly on the word where they have made mistakes if there are any. They then rewrite the word correctly. There is evidence for this practice (Templeton, 2011), and Mr. Piña notes that his students' spelling has really improved while he only devoted ten minutes per day to this learning. Tori is a student in the class and, when asked about it, said, "I like doing it this way. If we did it on paper, it would seem more serious. This way, we're just learning."

Mr. Piña also uses Kahoot in his class as another universal response opportunity, especially for mathematics. But, as he says, "I turn off the timer because I don't think it's about how fast they can answer. I want them to focus on accuracy." Mr. Piña uses a poll/re-poll approach in which students respond to the question, talk with a partner about the class results, and then take the poll again. As Mr. Piña notes, "The conversations about the responses that are not correct are really powerful. I think that when they analyze the errors that they think others have made, they really learn a lot."

REFLECT

Mr. Piña used two different universal response opportunities with his students. How often will you commit to providing this opportunity for your students? Which tools will you use to provide these opportunities?

Assessment using teach-back. Another way to embed assessment into instruction is through the use of a teach-back. Providing students opportunities to teach-back what they have learned is good for their learning, and it's a great opportunity for determining what has stuck and if there are any misconceptions. And this is not limited to in-class interactions. Students can teach their siblings, parents, or extended family members. They can teach-back to the class or directly to the teacher.

Another skill we have learned during distance learning is the usefulness of student digital recordings of their learning. The technology has advanced to the point where even young children can record themselves and submit their video to their class learning management system. In a teach-back video, students record themselves teaching someone else in their environment or submit an explanation to the class to view. These videos are short in length (less than three minutes) but hold a treasure trove of assessment information for you about their learning. Spread these out so that 25 percent of your students are submitting a short teach-back video each week. In four weeks' time, all of the students in the class will have completed one. These can be repurposed later for students to use again as an ipsative, or comparative, assessment (revisit Module 3 for more information on ipsative assessments). Here are a few examples of students teaching back that their teachers used as assessment information.

- A student in world history retold the major events of the French Revolution on video and included quiz questions for his peers.

- A student in geometry taught her sister how to determine the height of a right triangle.

- A student learning Spanish taught his parents the names of the eating utensils.

- A student records a video for her classmates about a picture book she recommends about community helpers.

Notice that these did not require instructional time. But they did provide the teacher an opportunity to notice what had been learned and if there were still things that needed to be learned. Of course, teachers can also arrange time during class for students to teach each other. The key is to ensure that the same students are not always doing the teach-back. Everyone needs an opportunity as it is good for learning and for assessment.

As an example, Somaya is a second grader who is learning English as an additional language. In her class, students use teach-back each week as one of the center rotations. Somaya has been learning about how sound is made. She prepared a lesson for her class that included the vocabulary words *pitch* and *volume*. With the help of her teacher, she recorded several different sounds made with vibrating objects and talked about the differences in pitch and volume. As her teacher noted, "It was a perfect lesson. She totally understands this content and I could see it. And I think her peers really learned a lot from her, too. But I know that I don't need to worry about her knowledge of sounds. She's got it and is ready to move on."

One simple teach-back that we can all use was also first implemented as part of distance learning. A group of teachers wanted to know if their students knew what they were supposed to be learning. As we noted in Module 5, clarity of the learning intentions is really important. Students need to know what they are learning and what success looks like. We developed three questions useful in increasing the clarity of lessons:

- What am I learning today?

- Why am I learning this?

- How will I know that I learned it? (Fisher et al., 2016, p. 27)

To determine whether or not students knew the answers, their teachers asked them to record quick videos answering each question. Their responses are like exit slips that allow teachers to see if students know what they are learning or if they are confused. And they allow teachers to get a sense of their students' perceptions of relevance as well as their definitions of success. Together, these make for valuable ways to assess students' understanding.

Assessment through writing. Writing is also a powerful way to assess students' learning. When students write, they think. Thus, writing provides a glimpse into students' thinking about the content. Of course, writing is also its own subject and can be taught and assessed in and of itself. As we note below, writing is a skill that is likely to be highly affected by online teaching.

Typically, students write in response to a prompt that is compared with a rubric or checklist. Unfortunately, this is an area that likely needs more attention. It seems that writing volume has declined during distance learning and that writing was less likely to be the focus of instruction. To be sure, there were teachers who engaged students in writing. But writing well is hard and likely needs to be something we all attend to. Short constructed responses in the form of daily exit tickets provide the students with opportunities to rehearse and retrieve newly learned skills and concepts. Think of this as a form of low-stakes practice. Regular rehearsal and retrieval are crucial for learning new information, and repeated use forms memory traces in the brain (Roediger & Karpicke, 2006). Even better, students can rate their level of confidence about their learning of the day's material by using a scale:

1. I am not sure of this and need more instruction.

2. I am learning this but need more practice.

3. I can do this independently.

4. I can teach someone else about this.

In doing so, you get immediate feedback from your students about where they are in their learning and can make timely adjustments, including meeting up with the group who indicated that they needed some re-teaching. There is the added benefit to them in terms of their agency, as they link their current level of understanding to their next steps and actions. Finally, your responsiveness to them signals your caring and support for their learning.

Co-constructing rubrics. Assessment is more than just measuring student learning. In fact, it is part of the learning activity itself, and students should be involved in all phases, including design (Boud, 2010). Promote engagement and deepen their learning by co-constructing major rubrics with your students. Constructing a rubric with students begins with the success criteria for the project. In many cases, you may have an existing rubric that you have used, and this can be a launching point for refining the rubric. For example, you may start with a rubric that will be used throughout the course, such as a rubric for a science lab

PAUSE & PONDER

Consider the prior experiences you have had with using flexible assessments. Use the scale to identify if this is an area of needed growth (red) through strength (green). Where do you fall on each of these actions? How could you apply these approaches in your class?

FLEXIBLE ASSESSMENT APPROACH	LEVEL OF PRIOR EXPERIENCE	APPLICATION TO YOUR CLASS
Universal responses		
Teach-back		
Writing		
Co-constructing rubrics		

Prioritize. Which of the above actions would you like to change? Highlight the one that you want to change and describe below what you will do to create that change:

report or an argumentative essay. This can be coupled with anonymous student examples from prior years in order to get their advice about what could have been done to improve the assignment. In doing so, you can capture the language of your students as they describe the components, as many rubrics are written with an adult audience in mind, rather than a student one. In the process, students gain a deeper understanding of the way their work will be assessed.

CONFIRMATIVE ASSESSMENTS TO GAUGE IMPACT

The bookend to an initial assessment is one that confirms learning has occurred. These assessments are used to gauge proficiency and mark a continued trajectory of competence, as well as a signal when further intervention is warranted. Successful learning recovery requires that student progress, as well as achievement, are closely monitored. A significant blind spot emerges when achievement alone is the only data that are examined. A list of scores on a confirmative assessment, such as an end-of-unit test, tells you nothing about student progress or your impact. Is it possible that some students were already well on their way to mastery at the beginning of the unit and made little growth during the unit? Are there students who knew little at the beginning but made a learning leap, even though they didn't quite reach mastery? Who knows? Without a means for comparing an initial assessment to a confirmative assessment, these questions cannot be answered.

There is much at stake for teacher and student when these questions remain. For teachers, there can be a significant loss of agency and self-efficacy. Without evidence of a positive impact due to their instruction, the only conclusion left to draw is that too many students didn't achieve mastery and therefore, the teacher isn't effective. Remember that reliance on partial information is an assessment bias. Students who only see a final score are endangered because there is no way of knowing whether acceleration is occurring or not. Acceleration programs have an effect size of 0.68 (www.visiblelearningmexta.com). The reason we know that is because the effect size of the effort has been calculated. The good news is that you can find out which students are making progress and are therefore responding positively to instruction and which students are not yet making progress. Those students are a signal to the teacher that instruction needs to be more finely tuned to spur growth. To calculate your impact, use an Excel spreadsheet. Here's how:

1. Type the students' names in one column.

2. Type their initial and postassessments in the other columns.

3. Highlight the column with the preassessment scores and select the "average" tool and place the average at the bottom of that column.

4. Do the same for the postassessment column.

The next step in determining the effect size is to calculate standard deviation. Excel will do this as well:

5. Type =STDEV.P and then select the student scores in the preassessment column again.

6. Do the same in the postassessment column.

7. Subtract the preassessment from the postassessment and then divide by the average (of Steps 5 and 6) standard deviation. (You can quickly calculate standard deviation on a number of websites, such as graphpad .com/quickcalcs/CImean1.cfm.)

Here's the formula:

$$\text{Effect size} = \frac{\text{Average (postassessment)} - \text{Average (preassessment)}}{\text{Average standard deviation or SD}^*}$$

Another way to do this is to visualize the data. Start by downloading the progress versus achievement tool from Visible Learning+™, available at www.visiblelearning.com/resources. It can yield a graphic that looks like this:

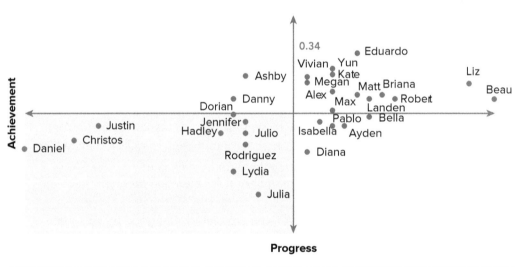

Reading Progress and Achievement

Source: Fisher, D., Frey, N., Almarode, J., Flories, K., & Nagel, D. (2020a). PLC+: Better decisions and greater impact by design. Corwin.

Based on this visualization of progress and achievement, several conclusions can be reached:

- **Upper-right quadrant: High Achievement/High Growth.** Students such as Eduardo, Yun, Kate, Liz, and Beau exceeded the achievement benchmark, represented by the horizontal line, but they also demonstrated high levels of progress, beyond average growth represented by the vertical line. The combination of high growth and high achievement is the desire of every stakeholder in education. In addition, they are accelerating in their learning.

- **Upper-left quadrant: High Achievement/Little Growth.** Ashby and Danny did not benefit from instruction during the unit but would otherwise go unnoticed because their achievement masked the fact that they did not learn. These students are decelerating in their learning.

- **Lower-right quadrant: Low Achievement/High Growth.** Find Diana, Bella, or Isabella on the grid. These students, along with Pablo and Ayden, showed high growth but did not cross the benchmark. In many schools, these learners would fall into the "did not pass" category and be assumed to be struggling students. However, a more purposeful analysis of who benefited and who did not benefit reveals that these learners demonstrated high growth. This fact alone indicates that these learners benefited greatly from instruction and that they demonstrated acceleration in their learning.

- **Lower-left quadrant: Low Achievement/Little Growth.** Daniel, Julia, Lydia, and others showed no growth and minimal achievement. In fact, many of the learners in this quadrant showed negative growth. What was it about this particular unit of instruction that there was little impact in growth and achievement for Daniel, Julia, Lydia, and the others? These students are decelerating in their learning.

To know one's impact is to understand what instructional processes are accelerating learning and for whom. In the case of students who are not demonstrating growth, it is an opportunity to calibrate and fine-tune learning so that students can gain ground. The question is this: Are you willing to use assessment data to improve your impact?

SPRING FORWARD

Acceleration is essential to engage in learning leaps, and assessment drives many of the decisions that teachers make. This requires a new mindset for assessment that begins with back-to-school measures to quickly gauge where students are. We don't need to squander weeks to find out where the gaps are. Assessments need to be shorter and more frequent so that we can pivot more quickly when students are not making progress. And finally, we need to gauge our own impact so that we can respond equally as well to students who achieve but do not progress, as well as students who are neither achieving nor progressing. Most importantly, we also need to celebrate those students who are blossoming!

REFLECT

Reflect on your learning about learning leaps and assessment efforts. Identify actions you are considering based on your learning.

IMPORTANT

On a scale of 1 to 5, with 5 being very important and 1 being not important at all, how would you rate the value of assessment efforts in your classroom or school?

1   2   3   4   5

WAIT, BUT WHY?

Explain your reason for the rating above.

MODULE 7

RECOVERING LEARNING THROUGH SUPPORTIVE SCHOOLWIDE SYSTEMS

The twin pandemics of disease and social injustice have exposed inequities in schooling that have existed all along. We have spent these last months understanding who the most vulnerable students are. Students who disappeared because they didn't have adequate access to technology. Those whose families suffered economic and personal loss. Children who were not able to fully benefit from special education services. Young people whose mental health and well-being has suffered.

We can take a lesson from an institution that regularly deals with disaster— the hospital. Emergency rooms in hospitals prepare in advance for the arrival of those patients who will need the highest level of care. They don't just wait idly at the door for the next ambulance to pull up. Recovering learning requires more than relying on the same systems we have used in the past. We have a good indication of who is likely to need more specialized supports. We can't afford to wait to see who might arrive at the school door and then scramble around for supports. Like a well-equipped hospital, we need systems of support to care for the academic, social and emotional, and mental health of students. To do so requires that we redirect resources to meet the specialized needs of those in jeopardy. Teachers can accomplish much with students, but they can't do it alone. Let's reevaluate the systems we have to support their learning recovery.

WHAT YOU'LL LEARN

LEARNING INTENTIONS

- I am learning about the role of systems in preparing for the academic and social and emotional needs of students who require more support.

- I am learning about systems for responding to chronic absenteeism in our return to school.

- I am learning about systems for anticipating increased mental health needs of students.

- I am learning about systems for anticipating increased online credit recovery needs.

- I am learning about systems for anticipating possible compensatory education services.

SUCCESS CRITERIA

- I can critically examine current support systems to identify strengths and gaps.

- I can redesign systems to anticipate new academic and social and emotional needs as students return to school.

SELF-ASSESSMENT

Use the provided scale to identify your level of knowledge about systems of support for returning students. Consider each of these statements:

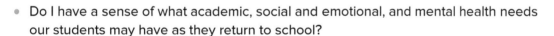

- Do I have a sense of what academic, social and emotional, and mental health needs our students may have as they return to school?

- Am I knowledgeable about the current status of our systems?

- Am I confident that proactive systems have been designed to respond to these needs?

HOW DO WE PREPARE FOR WHAT IS NEXT?

We are not certain about how much learning recovery needs to be made and by whom. There are students whose performance or understanding has been compromised. Yet there are other students who performed well, even better than in their past. The predictions from some scholarly organizations, such as the "COVID slide" projected by the Annenberg Institute at Brown University (Kuhfeld et al., 2020a) of 32 percent to 37 percent in reading and 50 percent to 63 percent in mathematics, have been challenged by large-scale data presented by groups such as NWEA. Their 4.4 million MAP assessments of Grades 3 to 8 show relatively little loss for those who took the assessment (Kuhfeld et al., 2020b). But there is solemn news within those findings. Up to 25 percent of the students who took the test in 2019 did not do so in 2020. Many of those students were from low-income households, often Black or Latinx. While some students did well, others fell further behind. In many school systems, existing equity gaps further widened. The distribution of learning, and learning recovery needs, has not been even. It never was pre-pandemic.

But here's what we do know—there are students in each and every school that have disproportionately suffered. In some places, the numbers will be larger; in other places, smaller. But every school will have some. To bury our heads in the sand and refuse to prepare for what lies ahead does an enormous disservice to communities, families, students, and ourselves. We need to marshal the capital we have as schools to respond effectively.

THERE ARE STUDENTS IN EACH AND EVERY SCHOOL THAT HAVE DISPROPORTIONATELY SUFFERED.

The key message is do not assume—diagnose, discover, investigate the status of learning for every student. Do not assume that those who are behind are only the naughty or disruptive students, and that the advanced and gifted students performed just fine. Check with every student. And check a broad spectrum from achievement, interest and motivation, angst and loneliness, health and happiness. All are part of learning, and all could be affected (positively or negatively) by COVID at-home teaching and learning.

Every school possesses varying levels of three kinds of capital: social capital, professional capital, and decisional capital (Hargreaves & Fullan, 2012). Social capital refers to the relational trust among adults in the school and is necessary for communication. Professional capital refers to the technical skills and qualifications of the adults at the school. And decisional capital refers to the empowerment of teams to take consequential action. Responding to the anticipated needs of students requires that all three types of capital are in adequate supply.

Another institution that thinks a lot about capital of a different sort is the banking industry. In the aftermath of the financial crisis of 2007–2009, banks are now required to undergo periodic stress tests. Bank managers run various scenarios to see if their institution can withstand economic stress and to test its strength. Let's do that with our schools. For the sake of argument, let's use that same figure of missing students in the fall 2020 NWEA assessment cycle: 25 percent. Calculate the number of students in your school to determine what 25 percent means. Now use that number to assess whether you currently have adequate capital in place to serve that volume of students.

An Educational Institution Stress Test

STRESS ITEM	YES	NO
1. Twenty-five percent of your students were *chronic absentee* problems in this past school year. Do you have a system in place to re-engage them in coming back to school?		
2. Twenty-five percent of your students need *social and emotional* or *behavioral* supports that require supplemental (Tier 2) or intensive (Tier 3) supports. Can you accommodate them?		
3. Twenty-five percent of your students are demonstrating *mental health* concerns that require counseling. Can the counselors at the school serve that number of students?		
4. Twenty-five percent of your students have suffered trauma that requires the support of a *social worker*. Do you have the capacity to serve students and their families?		
5. Twenty-five percent of your secondary students did not make adequate progress and will need to *repeat at least one course*. Do you have teaching staff to accommodate the expansion?		
6. Twenty-five percent of your students with disabilities need further *compensatory education* to meet their learning goals. Can the educational specialists take on an increased caseload?		
TOTAL		

MODULE 7

Interpret your results based on the number of items you answered as NO. This will yield a Sensitivity to Risk score.

0–1 Nos: You are in a strong position and are well-capitalized.

2–3 Nos: You are in a satisfactory position and are adequately capitalized.

4–5 Nos: You are in a flawed position and are undercapitalized.

6 Nos: You are in a critical position and are significantly undercapitalized.

Schools will need an apparatus of supportive systems to move students forward in their learning. In this module, we explore systems changes that can make a difference for students and educators. We will begin with redefining engagement with teachers.

REDEFINING ENGAGEMENT SCHOOLWIDE

Ask most educators what they have been most concerned about in this unsettled school year and they will immediately answer, "Engagement." But what does engagement really mean? When asked, many teachers immediately talk about behavioral engagement, particularly having cameras on. We certainly understand the need to see students (we're teachers, too), and it is a bit unnerving to teach to ceiling fans and little black boxes on a screen. But the reasons for having a camera off are more complex than a compliance mindset suggests. Some students didn't want to reveal the circumstances of where they were learning from. Imagine having the whole class drop into your home or apartment to look around. Some students spent their learning days inside of cars or bundled up from the cold outside on picnic tables near free Wi-Fi.

And let's not forget how unsettling it is to look at all of your classmates nonstop and having everyone look at you. Many students, especially older ones, report that they don't like their appearance. Social media promotes impossible beauty standards and many students are accustomed to using filters to enhance their visual image. Any wonder that they want their cameras off? It isn't about you. Stop taking it personally.

Let's begin with a schoolwide reset with educators about what engagement really means. Rather than a simplistic engaged/disengaged dichotomy that doesn't serve teachers or students very well, Amy Berry (2020) sought to develop a continuum of engagement that assumed (1) engagement can vary throughout a lesson; and (2) there is a relationship among engagement, motivation, and learning. Working with teachers, she developed a continuum of engagement that is more holistic and especially takes the degree of learning into account.

A Continuum of Engagement

ACTIVE ← ——————————————— PASSIVE ——————————————— → ACTIVE

Disrupting	Avoiding	Withdrawing	Participating	Investing	Driving
Distracting others Disrupting the learning	Looking for ways to avoid work Off-task behavior	Being distracted Physically separating from group	Doing work Paying attention Responding to questions	Asking questions Valuing the learning	Setting goals Seeking feedback Self-assessment

DISENGAGEMENT	ENGAGEMENT

Source: Berry, A. (2020). Disrupting to driving: Exploring upper primary teachers' perspectives on student engagement. *Teachers and Teaching, 26*(2), 145–165. doi:10.1080/13540602.2020.1757421

You'll notice that passivity is in the center of the continuum. Withdrawing is the first degree of disengagement, while participating is the first degree of engagement. Berry noted that participating correlated only to the surface level of learning and did not result in the kind of deep learning needed for students to flourish. As she said, there is a difference between "engagement in school and engagement in learning" (p. 160). The Participating level describes general teacher-pleasing behaviors. To be engaged in learning, students need to be at the levels of Investing (asking questions, valuing learning) and Driving (setting goals, seeking feedback, and self-assessing). If the latter sounds familiar, good! This highest level of engagement requires that teachers create opportunities for students to drive their own learning. And these opportunities foster student agency in learning.

THERE IS A DIFFERENCE BETWEEN "ENGAGEMENT IN SCHOOL AND ENGAGEMENT IN LEARNING."

Many teachers we know have used this engagement continuum with their students during distance learning. They co-construct working definitions with their students on each of these levels and provide students with self-assessment opportunities at the end of lessons. This practice should be continued and expanded as we collectively work to address learning loss and re-engagement. The levels of engagement are not limited to distance learning and can be applied to just about any format of schooling. The key lesson learned during COVID teaching was to have students define "engagement" and then reflect on their level of engagement following each lesson. When students understand what engagement looks like, they can make decisions and reflect on their actions.

MODULE 7

How can you create opportunities for students to drive their learning? We have started a list for you. What other ideas can you add?

Feedback. Teachers provide students with feedback and scaffold the process of students seeking feedback.	• Feedback is process related. • Feedback is about self-regulation. • Feedback is timely. • •
Goal setting. Teachers help students set goals to complete coursework while improving agency.	• Goals are mastery oriented. • Goal setting occurs weekly. • Students have opportunities to monitor and reflect on progress toward goals. • •
Self-assessment. Teachers design assessments that require student agency.	• Students self-assess at the beginning of a unit of instruction. • Students self-assess based on success criteria. • Students have opportunities to do comparative self-assessments. • •

ATTENDANCE AND CHRONIC ABSENTEEISM

There has been a shift in the last decade to more fully understanding chronic absenteeism and tardiness and methods for addressing it. Although some absences are due to truancy without the knowledge of a parent, students are more likely to be absent with the parent's permission. Every day that is missed is a day of learning that is lost. And we should start framing it this way for students and their families. Rather than saying "Your child is absent," perhaps we should say "Today was a day of learning lost" so that we collectively acknowledge the impact that missing school has on learning. Of course, there are valid reasons to stay away from school, which have been highlighted in public health communications. But some students are absent a lot.

Chronic absenteeism is defined as missing at least 10 percent of the school year for any reason, including those days of learning lost that are excused by the parent. While rates of chronic absenteeism are highest for high school students, the pattern of being absent from school can begin in the primary grades. There is an echo effect in that chronically absent students may also be chronically tardy students who are habitually late to schools and classes. The effects of chronic absenteeism are associated with lower academic achievement and test scores and an increased likelihood that the student will drop out of school altogether (Balfanz & Byrnes, 2012).

Less well-known is the spillover effect that chronically absent or tardy students have on their classmates. Kindergartners in classes with chronically tardy students had lower individual social and emotional outcomes, particularly in the areas of self-control, with more behavior problems, and lower interpersonal skills (Gottfried, 2014). Third- and fourth-grade classmates of chronically absent students showed lower academic achievement levels on standards-based tests of reading and math (Gottfried, 2019). There is a toll on their teachers as well, who lose valuable instructional and planning time (Musser, 2011).

WE HAVE LEARNED MUCH FROM DISTANCE LEARNING, AND WE NEED TO CAPITALIZE ON THAT TO SERVE STUDENTS MORE ABLY.

There are many factors that can contribute to chronic absenteeism, but in the context of the pandemic, the disruptions to the family's social fabric cannot be discounted. Families stretched thin to ensure that their children were attending distance or hybrid learning could not always do so. In many cases, older siblings had to supervise the schooling of younger children, thus sacrificing their own in the process. The economic losses suffered by families resulted in adolescents taking jobs to financially contribute. Other students all but disappeared from schooling due to mental health issues. While there are no firm data to date, there is intense speculation in the psychiatric community that prolonged isolation, stress, and trauma will negatively impact the post-disaster mental health recovery of adolescents (Guessoum et al., 2020). Regardless of where your school is in the process of returning to in-person learning, your students may be experiencing these challenges.

In other cases, you will have some students who did well in distance learning and now face a decline in their attendance and achievement upon returning to school. For some students, the higher degree of freedom to self-pace or to escape a bullying climate reduced their anxiety level and improved their learning. In going forward, attendance and learning problems for these students can and should include hybrid or fully distance learning options at their home school, not at another specialized school. We have learned much in a season of distance learning, and we need to capitalize on what we have learned to serve students more ably.

Interestingly, socialization can prove to be an antidote to chronic absenteeism. Contact with classmates is a major source of socialization. In one study of chronic absenteeism and unexcused absences in elementary, the presence of familiar faces reduced the likelihood of either (Kirksey & Gottfried, 2018). In other words, in classrooms that had a higher percentage of classmates from the previous school year, familiar faces served as a protective factor. The researchers speculated that this class composition has a positive effect of "self-concept and peer stability . . . and may contribute to consistency in the schooling environment" (p. 236). One possible consideration is to locate chronically absent students in classrooms with some classmates from two years ago or the last documented school year where the student experienced in-person learning.

There has been other promising work on re-engaging students who are chronically absent in the form of school teams. The Early Warning Intervention (EWI) team model consists of a multidisciplinary team of academic and non-academic personnel (Davis et al., 2019). The team is led by an adult in the school who serves as a facilitator for team meetings and a central figure for coordinated communication. In addition, there is a member of the team who can serve as a liaison between home and school. This person might be a full-time parent education coordinator, or the role might be spread among several school members assigned by grade level. Unlike other models, re-engagement is not the sole responsibility of those one or two people. Rather, every adult in the school is a potential member, depending on the student. These teams meet biweekly to discuss interventions, progress, and barriers across three markers called the ABCs: attendance, behavior, and course performance (Davis et al., 2019).

CASE IN POINT

The staff at Granger Middle School have reviewed the attendance data from the past year to identify students who were chronically absent. The intent is to proactively monitor students who are likely to continue struggling this school year. The EWI team constituted for Riley, a seventh-grade student who missed significant learning time the previous year, is led by Nathan Reynolds, the part-time attendance coach for the school, who facilitates the meetings. He is joined by Jordan Cabrera, the school social worker and parent liaison. Riley's core subject teachers are part of this team. Over the summer, Granger built an early warning system using their management information system (MIS) so that they can monitor her progress.

Attendance is entered daily for every student, as are referrals for problematic behavior and grades. They use a traffic light system to note when any student moves from green to yellow or red. The names of students of concern are sent to the administrator. The names of students on the EWI caseload are then sent to Mr. Reynolds, who coordinates the team meetings. Riley's name was forwarded because of concern about attendance. In the first twenty days of school, she has been absent four times, a rate of 20 percent. All of the absences were excused by the parent. There haven't been any behavioral concerns, but she already has a current grade of Incomplete in science and social studies, although she appears to be doing better in English and math.

REFLECT

Mr. Reynolds, the facilitator, is preparing questions for discussion with the team. What questions do you advise be posed to the teachers? What questions might Ms. Cabrera, the social worker, prepare for when she talks to Riley's family?

DISCUSSION QUESTIONS FOR RILEY'S TEACHERS	DISCUSSION QUESTIONS FOR RILEY'S FAMILY

SOCIAL AND EMOTIONAL LEARNING SUPPORTS

The social and emotional skills of students influence their ability to be able to make decisions, self-regulate their behavior and learning, and process their emotions. For some students, these skills have been negatively impacted and the return to school will be especially bumpy. Now more than ever, schools returning to face-to-face learning must consider how they will implement a schoolwide focus on social and emotional learning that includes both explicit instruction as well as SEL that is infused into the academic flow of the curriculum. The

Collaborative for Academic, Social, and Emotional Learning (CASEL) notes that quality indicators for schoolwide SEL include the following:

CLASSROOM		Explicit SEL Instruction	Students have consistent opportunities to cultivate, practice, and reflect on social and emotional competencies in ways that are developmentally appropriate and culturally responsive.
		SEL integrated with academic instruction	SEL objectives are integrated into instructional content and teaching strategies for academics as well as music, art, and physical education.
SCHOOL		Youth voice and engagement	Staff honor and elevate a broad range of student perspectives and experiences by engaging students as leaders, problem solvers, and decision makers.
		Supportive school and classroom climates	Schoolwide and classroom learning environments are supportive, culturally responsive, and focused on building relationships and community.
		Focus on adult SEL	Staff have regular opportunities to cultivate their own social, emotional, and cultural competence, collaborate with one another, build trusting relationships, and maintain a strong community.
		Supportive discipline	Discipline policies and practices are instructive, restorative, developmentally appropriate, and equitably applied.
		A continuum of integrated supports	SEL is seamlessly integrated into a continuum of academic and behavioral supports, which are available to ensure that all student needs are met.
FAMILY		Authentic family partnerships	Families and school staff have regular and meaningful opportunities to build relationships and collaborate to support students' social, emotional, and academic development.
COMMUNITY		Aligned community partnerships	School staff and community partners align on common language, strategies, and communication around all SEL-related efforts and initiatives, including out-of-school time.
		Systems for continuous improvement	Implementation and outcome data are collected and used to monitor progress toward goals and continuously improve all SEL-related systems, practices, and policies with a focus on equity.

Source: CASEL. (2020). *The CASEL guide to schoolwide SEL essentials.* https://schoolguide.casel.org/resource/the-casel-guide-to-schoolwide-sel-essentials (p. 2)

The development of a quality schoolwide SEL plan requires an investment in the social, professional, and decisional capital of the adults at the school. CASEL recommends four areas of focus in order to implement SEL systemically (CASEL, 2020). Their guide for schoolwide SEL planning is available at schoolguide.casel.org:

- **Focus Area 1: Build foundational support and plan** by building awareness, consensus, and a shared vision.

- **Focus Area 2: Strengthen adult SEL** by developing the capacity of the staff to cultivate their own social, emotional, and cultural competence.

- **Focus Area 3: Promote SEL for students** such that it is infused into academic instruction, fosters student voice, and includes family and community partnerships.

- **Focus Area 4: Practice continuous improvement** through data-driven decisions about SEL goals and outcomes.

As a starting point for an SEL effort in classrooms, consider the unique developmental and learning needs for different age ranges of students you serve.

Primary students. Young children have less experience with face-to-face schooling and the organization of the classroom and school. Plan for additional instruction and time to develop these skills with these students. It can be expected that some students will revert to younger behaviors, especially as they learn again how to separate from their families each day. This should be of particular emphasis during the first month of school and should include regular revisiting of these skills. Consider how you will do the following:

- Co-constructing norms for the classroom

- Engaging in a morning welcoming routine that includes an emotional check-in

- Ending each day with a closing routine, such as a circle, that includes reflection, celebration, and a closing (Responsive Classroom, 2011)

> SOME STUDENTS WILL REVERT TO YOUNGER BEHAVIORS, ESPECIALLY AS THEY LEARN AGAIN HOW TO SEPARATE FROM THEIR FAMILIES EACH DAY.

Upper elementary students. Students in middle childhood are learning to engage in more sophisticated social relationships with peers, and these don't always go smoothly. You can assume that your students are a bit rusty at this and could use some extra support:

- Infuse your curriculum with texts and materials that are a gateway to conversations about how real and imagined people they are learning about make decisions that are moral and ethical.

- Establish processes for class meetings so that your students learn how to come together as a community to solve problems.

Middle school students. Early adolescence can be a time of great turmoil and is marked by a time of testing boundaries. Physical and emotional changes are as bewildering for them as they are for the adults who love them. Their relationships with one another, coupled with access to social media, can lead some of them to make decisions that hurt themselves and others:

- Teach a comprehensive antibullying approach that includes not only how to recognize it but also guidance on decision making and managing social conflict (Committee for Children, 2020). Consider infusing some into advisories, with other lessons taking place in content area classes.

- Create opportunities for greater student voice in the school on substantive matters. These might include establishing a principal's advisory, student representation at parent–teacher organization meetings, and student surveys about curriculum and school climate.

High school students. Many adolescents have faced increased responsibility at home as their families struggle economically and balance households with younger children in distance learning. Some have taken part-time jobs to sustain their family while others have provided home health care to sick relatives. Many have participated in protests about social injustices and have organized community responses. They are returning as young people who have assumed leadership roles in their families and communities. They have insistent questions about themselves and the world and are not willing to accept the status quo:

- Teach about organization and activism through curricular connections and specialized clubs.

- Create peer mentoring programs so that students can support their classmates emotionally and academically.

- Partner with community groups to develop service-learning opportunities.

MENTAL HEALTH SUPPORTS

The needs of some students for more intensive supports beyond Tier 1 SEL supports discussed previously is clear: We should fully anticipate that we will have students, including those not previously identified, who will need more intensive supports. The National Alliance on Mental Illness reports that 1 in 6 young people between the ages of six and seventeen will experience a mental illness and that 50 percent of lifetime mental illnesses begin by age fourteen (National Alliance on Mental Illness [NAMI], 2020). While depression rates among young people have risen steadily in the last decade, access to mental health services has not (Mojtabai et al., 2016). School counselors and school social workers are an integral part of a multitiered system of supports (MTSS) that includes supplemental interventions (Tier 2) such as small group counseling, as well as intensive interventions (Tier 3) that include short-term crisis counseling and monitoring student progress during postintervention (California Association of School Counselors, n.d.).

Two major problems exist in getting mental health supports to students: a lack of coordination of staffing and a lack of coordination inside of schools. To be clear, we believe that supports for schools need to include more staffing of specialists, including counselors and social workers. The American Association of School Counselors and the National Association of Social Workers recommends a ratio of 1 for every 250 students. In California, for example, the average is one counselor for every 626 students and one social worker for every 7,308 students (Lucile Packard Foundation for Children's Health, 2019). Fewer than 10 percent of students nationwide attend schools within the recommended ratio (Whitaker et al., 2018). Supports for students returning to school post-pandemic should include major legislative action to increase the number of mental health professionals in school districts.

However, increasing staffing will not address internal coordination problems. Without protocols for identifying and referring students who need supplemental or intensive supports, the continued problem of overreferral by some teachers and underreferrals by others will persist. You can begin by assessing your current referral management approach to identify and refer students who are of concern. Each of these steps is accompanied by self-assessment questions (Now Is the Time Technical Assistance Center, 2015). The complete tool kit, funded by the Substance Abuse and Mental Health Administration, can be downloaded at https://www.escneo.org/Downloads/NITT%20SMHRP%20Toolkit_11%2019%20 15%20FINAL.PDF.

PAUSE & PONDER

Mental health referral systems are only as good as the communication systems used to support them. Examine your school's current referral system for Tier 2 and Tier 3 mental and behavioral health supports. Use the traffic light scale to identify areas of strength and growth opportunities.

STAGE	SCHOOL SELF-ASSESSMENT QUESTIONS	HOW ARE WE DOING?
Establish a referral system	• Are systems in place for all types of referral concerns? • Are referral systems formalized? • Does a structure exist to manage referrals? • Are referral systems sensitive to developmental, cultural, and linguistic diversity?	
Manage referral flow	• Does the problem-solving team effectively collect initial referrals? • Does the problem-solving team effectively expand on initial referrals? • Does the problem-solving team have defined decision rules? • Does the problem-solving team have a record-management system?	

(Continued)

STAGE	SCHOOL SELF-ASSESSMENT QUESTIONS	HOW ARE WE DOING?
Map resources	• Has the team identified all school and community resources available to them? • Has the team examined the breadth and quality of interventions provided at school? • Has the team examined issues related to access to community-based resources?	
Evaluate intervention effectiveness	• What will it look like when this student no longer experiences the problem for which they were referred? • Does the problem-solving team collect process data? • Does the problem-solving team collect outcome data? • Does the problem-solving team monitor intervention progress? • Does the problem-solving team request intervention effectiveness information from community partners? • Does the problem-solving team request feedback from the student or his or her family about the intervention experience? • Has the problem-solving team adopted systems for tracking response to intervention? • Does the problem-solving team report intervention effectiveness information to stakeholders?	

REDEFINE CREDIT RECOVERY IN HIGH SCHOOL

In an effort to reclaim lost time for students who are not on track for graduation, a large number of high schools are utilizing online credit recovery courses. In pre-pandemic schooling, students completed self-paced online asynchronous courses in a face-to-face environment. These classrooms featured a dozen or more students on individual laptops moving through off-the-shelf courses featuring recorded lectures; short, assigned readings; and frequent assessments. One or two adults monitor course progress, render technical assistance, and provide additional content instruction as needed.

In reality, these credit recovery courses have delivered low rates of completion, usually between 30 percent to 55 percent (Heinrich et al., 2019). Students in ninth and tenth grade are even less likely to complete courses, compared to eleventh and twelfth graders. The difficulties of these younger students have been attributed to lower reading ability, lack of motivation and self-regulation to work alone, and more distraction. In addition, the implementation of an online credit recovery program can result in and amplify inequities. The likelihood that a student will take a credit recovery course increases by 15 percent each time they are suspended (Heinrich et al., 2019).

There is promise in utilizing online credit recovery courses in a blended environment, especially in the self-paced nature of the course. "Moonlighters" (students who complete 80% or more of the course outside the school day) are able to take advantage of the more flexible scheduling that an online course can offer. They spend more time in active course sessions, at 100 minutes. However, moonlighters, compared to other credit recovery classmates, are the least likely to qualify for free/reduced lunch rates or have a disability. They are also "the most academically prepared for online course taking" in terms of self-regulation skills and reading levels (Heinrich et al., 2019, p. 2171).

The quality of supports needed to ensure that students already falling behind in graduation credits must be increased, in acknowledgment that these students have already demonstrated that they are academically at risk. These supports reside primarily in the social and professional capital of the teachers charged with supporting students in credit recovery. These recommendations are drawn from the works of Darling-Aduana et al. (2019) and Heinrich et al. (2019).

Online Credit Recovery Program

How are the credit recovery courses at your school staffed, managed, and implemented to increase success? These indicators are drawn from research on course implementation of more than 20,000 course takers over a 4-year span at 46 high schools.

STAFFING: TEACHERS ASSIGNED	YES	NO	COURSE DESIGN	YES	NO
Possess content expertise in the subject of the online course.			Ninth- and tenth-grade students are not assigned to online credit recovery.		
Have received specific professional learning in supporting credit recovery students.			Students with disabilities are assigned to online courses aligned to the accommodations they need to be successful.		
Use technology tools to monitor progress and intervene when a student is stalled.			Class sizes are in line with other face-to-face courses in the school.		
Are not substitute teachers (engagement with students drops significantly when a substitute teacher runs the credit recovery class).			Students can access online credit recovery courses outside of the school day. The school has a process for determining that students have the technology to access it, and if they do not, the school provides access.		
IN-PERSON COURSE SUPPORTS	**YES**	**NO**	**MONITORING**	**YES**	**NO**
Live teacher interactions take place regularly to build and maintain trusting relationships with students.			Students who are consistently not making progress in online credit recovery courses are reassigned to a setting where they can receive more in-person instruction and support, rather than languishing.		

IN-PERSON COURSE SUPPORTS	YES	NO	MONITORING	YES	NO
Weekly progress goals are set with students, and weekly one-to-one conferences are held with the teacher to foster agency.			Students with other mental health, social and emotional, or behavioral support needs receive them as part of a comprehensive plan for their success.		
Student note-taking occurs and notes are checked by the teacher before course assessments.			Course progress and completion rates are part of schoolwide programmatic monitoring.		
When a student consistently fails to meet progress goals, the course is temporarily disabled so that the student must meet with the teacher before it is restarted.			Student demographics of who is taking and completing/not completing online credit recovery courses are monitored for structural and institutional barriers.		

BASED ON YOUR PROGRAM ASSESSMENT, WHAT AREAS NEED TO BE IMPROVED?

Staffing	Course design

In-person course supports	Monitoring

MODULE 7

COMPENSATORY EDUCATION SERVICES

Perhaps, one of the most challenging aspects of distance learning has been in serving some students with disabilities. Early on in the pandemic, it was quite difficult to deliver related services such as speech/language therapy and occupational therapy to students. These interruptions to specialized service delivery were eventually rectified for many using some creative technology workarounds, but others have remained quite challenging, such as physical therapy. In other cases, the lack of face-to-face instruction may have caused a regression. Whether related services or face-to-face instruction, the focus of compensatory instruction is not on whether progress slowed but whether there was a reversal. Compensatory services education is part of the law related to free and appropriate education (FAPE).

IF WE FAIL TO UNDERSTAND ENGAGEMENT AS ANYTHING MORE THAN A PUSH-AND-PULL PROCESS THAT HOLDS COMPLIANCE IN HIGHER ESTEEM THAN LEARNING, WE WILL FAIL TO REACH STUDENTS WHO ALREADY HAVE A FRAGILE RELATIONSHIP TO SCHOOLING.

As of this writing, compensatory services are still up in the air. However, existing regulations and case law state that compensatory education is warranted when a student with a disability has lost skills or regressed on individualized education program (IEP) goals because special education services were interrupted. Not every student with a disability warrants compensatory education. However, the current direction for determining the need for possible compensatory education is that districts collaborate with parents to jointly decide if and when it will be completed. Compensatory education can be offered during or after the school day, as well as in summer school. We know that's pretty nebulous information; our point is that in the return to school, how compensatory education determinations will be made is of primary concern. In advance of more specific directives from federal and state agencies, schools can act proactively to examine the progress of each student with a disability. The Colorado Department of Education recommends that these factors be considered in determining the need for compensatory services for disruption of FAPE (2020):

- Rate of progress on IEP goals prior to closure/disruption;

- Difference between IEP progress-monitoring data immediately preceding closure/disruption and IEP progress-monitoring data collected a reasonable time after the return to in-person instruction;

- Difference between services identified on the IEP and services offered during closure/disruption, including amount, frequency, duration, type, and delivery model;

- Accessibility of services offered to the student during closure/disruption;

- Changes in the general education curriculum, as well as level and type of instruction for all students during closure/disruption; and

- Input and information from parents concerning student performance during closure/disruption. (¶5)

How compensatory services are provided also varies considerably. These can include extra related services sessions conducted in person or intensive one-to-one or small group tutoring. In other cases, parents may be given funds to use for services not provided by the school (e.g., therapeutic camp). To be sure, this is an uncertain time and the pathway to do so is not at all clear. However, keep in mind that the relationship between school and home is central to this process. There is much in the way of goodwill and trust-building that can result from proactively examining student progress toward IEP goals and initiating conversations with families.

 CASE IN POINT

The special education team at Longacre Elementary is anticipating a return to face-to-face instruction and is looking forward to welcoming back their students. The school has always valued home-school connections in the small rural community they reside in. During the pandemic, they closed and opened several times but were able to close the school year with hybrid instruction. Distance learning was an option for the entire year, and many students with and without disabilities opted for doing so. The provision of related services was challenging, but in most cases, they were able to work out the kinks. The school designed a Google form during the early days of the school closure in order to keep track of contacts remotely (see Figure 12). "This was pretty difficult for us to manage last spring," said special educator Rose Callahan. "But we all agreed a few months back that this is one of the things we want to keep moving forward," she said. "It has proven to be a great way for us to communicate with one another."

Figure 12 (Name)'s Learning Continuity and Attendance Plan

Date	Duration	Staff	Instruction Provided and Format	Skill Area Addressed	Specific IEP Goal Data	Absent? (If so, log three contact attempts)	Notes (e.g., tasks or assessments completed, technology needs, social and emotional needs)

Source: Fisher, D., Frey, N., Law, N., & Smith, D. (2020). *On-your-feet guide: Distance learning for instructional leaders.* Corwin.

The team has now assembled because they want to go through each student's current IEP goals and compare them to the notes they gathered during distance and hybrid learning. "We want to keep lines of communication open with families," said Ms. Callahan. They have consulted the latest recommendations from their special education local plan area (SELPA) about compensatory services. The first thing they plan to do is to examine whether the time designated on the IEP was realized in their contact logs. Next, they want to spotlight students who may have lost skills during that time. "There are a couple of kiddos that we are concerned about," she said. They're in fact-finding mode right now and want to gather some early information.

REFLECT

Help the team prepare questions they will ask their students' general education teachers and the parents of the children to gain a preliminary sense of where compensatory services might be appropriate.

QUESTIONS TO ASK THE GENERAL EDUCATION TEACHERS	QUESTIONS TO ASK PARENTS OF STUDENTS WITH DISABILITIES

SPRING FORWARD

Re-engaging students with their learning requires two distinct moves on the part of schools. The first is to fundamentally redefine what engagement means. If we fail to understand engagement as anything more than a push-and-pull process that holds compliance in higher esteem than learning, we will fail to reach students who already have a fragile relationship to schooling. The second move is to critically examine existing systems meant to support these students—socioemotionally and academically—and locate those gaps in our systems. We already have a good sense of who those students are that will need more specialized support. Waiting for them to fail to attend, to make up lost academic progress, and to develop coping skills for the traumas they have experienced is institutionally negligent.

Our schools are filled with caring educators who are in this profession to make a positive difference in the lives of young people. But they cannot do that in isolation. By calibrating schoolwide systems to meet our students' needs, we empower educators to do so.

REFLECT

Reflect on your learning about systems of support for the academic and social and emotional needs of students as they return to school. Identify actions you are considering based on your learning.

IMPORTANT

On a scale of 1 to 5, with 5 being very important and 1 being not important at all, how would you rate the value of addressing the systems in your school for responding to these needs?

1   2   3   4   5

WAIT, BUT WHY?

Explain your reason for the rating above.

MODULE 8

LEARNING LEAPS THAT MOBILIZE INTERVENTION EFFORTS

If the systems we described in Module 4 are implemented, and students experience coordinated curriculum, instruction, and assessment, many (or even most) will experience the type of acceleration that we have been talking about. These processes and procedures will generally address any learning recovery that needs to occur as well as ensure that any content that was missed is taught.

But there are some students that will need significantly more academic attention to be successful. For these students, educators must allocate additional time and resources. This group of students needs their learning to take bigger leaps ahead. Beyond acceleration, there are some students who need a much more aggressive and systematic approach to their learning needs.

Generally, these efforts are known as response to intervention (RTI) with several tiers of action based on the needs of the student. Overall, RTI efforts have an effect size of 1.09, a very strong impact on learning. But only when they are implemented well. Simply calling something "RTI" doesn't make it so.

It's important to identify students who need intervention support and to design experiences that ensure that these leaps occur. We chose the phrase learning leaps because leaps are big efforts, with great force, that allow the person to reach a new height. What a great way to think about the efforts we can mobilize to help students who are in the most need.

WHAT YOU'LL LEARN

LEARNING INTENTIONS

- I am learning how to design and implement learning leaps.

SUCCESS CRITERIA

- I can determine the types of screening tools useful in my class or school.
- I can develop progress-monitoring systems.
- I can design effective tutoring programs.
- I can ensure students who need supplemental and intensive interventions receive them.

SELF-ASSESSMENT

Using the provided scale, identify your level of knowledge about addressing learning recovery through the curriculum. Consider each of these statements:

- I am aware of the intervention efforts available to my students.

- I have access to tutoring for my students.

- I know which students need supplemental and intensive interventions.

- I can allocate time to ensure that students receive the necessary interventions.

INTERVENTION AND OPPORTUNITIES TO LEARN

When students don't learn, despite really good planning and delivery, teachers who understand RTI respond. Unfortunately, in some places, the only response *is* intervention. It is true that some students need intervention, and this module includes information about supplement and intensive interventions. *But* sometimes learning leaps also require removing barriers and providing students increased opportunities to learn.

> WHEN STUDENTS DON'T LEARN, DESPITE REALLY GOOD PLANNING AND DELIVERY, TEACHERS WHO UNDERSTAND RTI RESPOND.

When teachers identify potential barriers and then work to remove them, students are more likely to respond to the quality core instruction that is provided and perhaps not even require interventions. However, barriers at the classroom level prevent students from fully benefiting from otherwise sound instruction. For example, some students are called on less frequently than others, often based on their current level of performance. In addition, some of these barriers are more systemic in nature, such as how schedules and course progressions are implemented. We have already discussed the impact of teacher expectations on students' learning as well as the use of instruction minutes. In this module, we'll focus on the interactions that teachers have with students.

Similarly, when teachers and schools provide opportunities for students to learn, learning can be enhanced. The opportunity to learn is "the degree to which a student experiences classroom instruction, including a variety of approaches that address a range of cognitive processes, teaching practices, and grouping formats" (Heafner & Fitchett, 2015, p. 228). For example, as we noted previously, the ways in which teachers group students can impact the opportunities they have. Likewise, the tasks that are assigned can be different in complexity across classes at the same school and across schools in the district. In addition to removing barriers and enhancing opportunities to learn, there are times when students need additional support, through systematic and intentional interventions, to acquire the necessary skills and concepts.

Taken together, removing barriers, providing opportunities to learn, and enhancing delivery interventions provide students with a responsive system that ensures that impact is realized. And it is *system* that is the important word. Too often, these three elements are disconnected from one another, and their potential for impact is lessened as a result. By creating a network of responses, rather than just one, we unleash the potential of RTI as a crucial part of school improvement and student success.

UNIVERSAL SCREENING AND ONGOING ASSESSMENT

In districts and schools that successfully engage students in intervention efforts, all students are initially assessed to determine who might need supplemental or intensive interventions right away. These screening tools should be quick and fairly easy to use because they are going to be administered to all students. As such, these tools are not expected to be diagnostic and might unintentionally identify students who really do not need an intervention; a screening tool merely identifies students who are working below grade level. These tools cannot assess what has been tried in the past and whether it has been successful or not. It is common to use student writing, encoding (spelling) inventories, and general math skills as screening tools. Regardless of the tools used, there must be a process in place to identify students in need of further investigation and possible intervention, and those interventions should begin within the first few weeks of the school year.

Most schools already have systems in place to identify needs. Remember visiting the nurse's office to have your hearing and vision checked? Covering one's eye and reading letters from a chart wasn't something to be embarrassed about; everyone was assessed with this tool. Whereas vision and hearing can be reasonably assessed less often,

> schoolwide screening is conducted to identify a subset of students whose response to Tier 1 general education is then monitored for a relatively short period of time to (dis)confirm the risk status indicated via schoolwide screening. Only the subset of students who (a) first meet the schoolwide screening cut point and (b) then evidence poor rates of improvement over five to eight weeks of Tier 1 general education are deemed in need of a preventative intervention.
>
> Our recommendation is that schools use schoolwide screening in combination with at least five weeks of weekly progress monitoring in response to general education to identify students who require preventative intervention. Our rationale is that one-time universal screening at the beginning of the year can over-identify students who require preventative intervention. (Fuchs & Fuchs, 2006, pp. 39–40)

There are a number of tools available to assess your school's efforts to organize and implement intervention.

The following activity includes a range of essential tasks for selecting and using screening tools. For your grade level, department, or school, who is responsible for each, and what is the status of implementation?

PAUSE & PONDER

In the second column, write the name(s) of the individual or team who will assume responsibility for the task identified in the first column. In the third column, write the deadline for or status of the task.

TASK	RESPONSIBLE INDIVIDUAL/TEAM	TIMELINE/STATUS
Once a tool has been selected, determine and secure the resources required to implement it.		
Determine initial professional development needs and continuing professional development support.		
Administer the screening measure three times a year (for example, early fall, midterm, and late spring).		
Create a database that aligns with the screening instrument to hold student information and scores.		
Organize the screening results (for example, graphs and tables) to provide a profile of all students and their comparisons with one another.		
Monitor results at the classroom level and make decisions about when teachers/instructional programs require more scrutiny and support.		
Add screening results to a database so that students' performance can be monitored over time.		
Specify written steps to follow when further scrutiny is needed for students judged to be at risk.		

Source: Johnson, E., Mellard, D. F., Fuchs, D., & McKnight, M. A. (2006). *Responsiveness to intervention (RTI): How to do it.* National Research Center on Learning Disabilities. https://files.eric.ed.gov/fulltext/ED496979.pdf. Used with permission.

REFLECT

What do you and your team need to put into place to ensure that all students are screened for potential intervention needs? How can a focus on learning leaps help your students?

PROGRESS MONITORING

Some students will perform well on the initial screening tools but need supplemental intervention later in the school year. Thus, schools also need systems to monitor the progress of learners, including the rate of learning and the level of performance. This is especially important now due to the potentially fractured nature of learning in the past year.

Progress monitoring informs the need for changes to instruction and potentially interventions as learners progress toward the learning intentions. Progress-monitoring tools are often forms of curriculum-based assessment, meaning that there is "direct observation and recording of a student's performance in the local curriculum as a basis for gathering information to make instructional decisions" (Deno, 1987, p. 41). These tools allow teachers to determine if students are making progress in the regular curriculum of the course, and the data can be used to inform the work of your team. The National Association of State Directors of Special Education (2005) identified nine essential characteristics for progress monitoring in an RTI system. Progress monitoring should do the following:

- Assess the specific skills embodied in state and local academic standards
- Assess marker variables that have been demonstrated to lead to the ultimate instructional target
- Be sensitive to small increments of growth over time
- Be administered efficiently over short periods
- Be administered repeatedly (using multiple forms)
- Result in data that can be summarized in teacher-friendly data displays
- Be comparable across students
- Be applicable for monitoring an individual student's progress over time
- Be relevant to the development of instructional strategies and use of appropriate curriculum that addresses the area of need (n.p.)

The National Center on Intensive Intervention provides an array of free, web-based progress-monitoring resource materials at https://intensiveintervention.org/intensive-intervention/progress-monitor.

There are a number of commercially available tools to monitor students' progress. Some schools develop course competencies based on the learning intentions and success criteria, or common formative assessments, that allow for an assessment of all students enrolled in a particular grade level or course. Students who do not demonstrate competency on one of these assessments are then provided with interventions at increasing levels of support, with teachers adjusting the intensity and duration of interventions based on the personalized needs of the student.

Competencies, or measures of proficiency, focus on the content that needs to be learned rather than the compliance activities that sometimes appear in grade books. As we have noted, it's important to monitor attendance and have systems in place to ensure that students don't have days of learning lost. But academic intervention should focus on what students need to learn. As examples of competencies,

- Students in science complete a project that demonstrates their understanding of the cellular structure
- Students in English write an essay in which they compare two pieces of literature against a set criterion
- Students in history engage in a debate that allows their teacher to assess their understanding of city-states
- Students in mathematics identify appropriate statistics to solve a research question
- Students in drama perform short monologues
- Students in physical education take a test on the rules of volleyball
- Students in reading retell a story they have read
- Students in social studies draw a map of their neighborhood

Notice that there are four major ways for students to demonstrate competency: projects, performances, essays, and tests. Of course, these need to be aligned with the standards for the subject area and should provide students an opportunity to demonstrate what they have learned.

Analysis of these competencies provides all teachers, not just English and math teachers, an opportunity to engage in intervention efforts. In many schools, students can only receive supplemental and intensive interventions based on their performance in reading or mathematics. In fact, nearly all formal progress-monitoring tools focus on reading and mathematics, meaning that other content areas are not reviewed. When teachers across the disciplines develop course competencies, progress monitoring occurs in every classroom, and every teacher becomes involved in the RTI process.

Note that we did not include homework as a trigger for intervention. In fact, homework is a fairly ineffective indicator of the need for intervention. Some students copy and appear proficient. Others don't do the homework because they know the content and believe that they will perform well on the assessments. Thus, homework should not be used for progress monitoring. Performance on curriculum-based measures is much more useful in allocating resources to intervention.

HOMEWORK IS A FAIRLY INEFFECTIVE INDICATOR OF THE NEED FOR INTERVENTION.

CASE IN POINT

Seyo is an eighth-grade student who performed generally well in seventh grade. Her school uses two screening tools at the start of the year: a math inventory developed by a local university and a writing assessment developed by the regional education system. Seyo performed about average on these assessments.

A few months into the year, Seyo did not demonstrate competence on her history exam. When she met with her teacher to discuss her performance, Seyo said that she was having a hard time reading the textbook and that there were a lot of words that she did not know. Her teacher, Matt Levine, suggested that she attend the learning lab after school so that they could work together on her knowledge and skills. The learning lab at her school is open every day, before and after school, and is staffed by different teachers each day.

Seyo attended these optional sessions after school for two weeks and still did not demonstrate proficiency. Mr. Levine decided to request more formal help from his grade-level team. Seyo's English teacher said that she was doing okay in class and her science teacher said that she passed the labs and struggled with the assessment. The team decided to change the focus of her intervention and give Seyo electronic practice versions of the assessments, in smaller chunks, that she could analyze with the instructors in the learning lab. The team realized a few things. First, Seyo was anxious about the tests and "froze up" when presented with the challenge. The practice tests helped her develop some confidence. Second, her vocabulary was somewhat limited, and the team had to figure out how to support her.

REFLECT

What do you recommend the team does to support Seyo's vocabulary needs? How did the use of competency-based assessment help the team allocate resources?

TUTORING

The use of tutoring to supplement core instruction is a longstanding practice in education. Tutoring can come in many forms, including peer tutoring (same age) and its variant, cross-age peer tutoring (older students working with younger ones), and there can be adult–student tutoring.

Tutoring by adults. The adults who provide tutoring services may be supplemental teachers funded via Title 1 or another source, paraprofessionals employed by the school, or student teachers assigned for their practicum. In other cases, they may be parent volunteers or out-of-school time educators in after-school programs. One of the most well-known tutoring efforts is Reading Recovery for first graders, who meet with highly trained interventionists for thirty minutes daily over a twelve-to-twenty-week time period. Well-designed tutoring initiatives have been demonstrated to be effective for elementary students in reading (Elbaum et al., 2000) and math (Slavin & Lake, 2008). A meta-analysis of adult tutoring of adolescents for literacy reported an effect size of 0.90, suggesting a high potential for accelerating learning (Jun et al., 2010).

A well-designed tutoring program should align with the same characteristics of a quality educational program. This includes

- A referral process for tutoring

- Clear objectives and outcomes

- A method for progress monitoring and reporting

- Communication systems that include the student's teacher and family

The tutors themselves should receive initial formal training as well as ongoing professional learning. A skilled supervisor or coordinator should be designated so that tutors can be supported and meet regularly to discuss successes and challenges.

We would recommend that when using adult tutors, we set the sessions as we would an IEP—making it clear what the focus of the tutoring is to be, the entry status of the student (or the tutor to help with this discovery), indications of instructional methods for tutoring (particularly if the tutor is not an ex-teacher), clarity about the success criteria of the tutoring, and demands to ensure there is convincing evidence of the improvement during the tutoring. This reduces a common negative about tutoring—that what is taught is not related to the classroom instruction. Asking the regular teacher to devise or sign off these plans increases the likelihood of the tutoring to accelerate the learning.

Intelligent tutoring systems. The exponential technology development of the last two decades has resulted in a large number of intelligent tutoring systems (ITS) that have become widely available to schools. With an effect size of 0.51, they are worth exploring to see if they might be useful in tutoring (Hattie, n.d.; www.visiblelearningmexta.com). These are one-to-one computer programs that begin with an initial diagnostic assessment to determine the student's current level of performance. Once assessed, the computer program adapts questions and provides feedback, hints, and prompts (Ma et al., 2014). There are several advantages to using an intelligent tutoring system. The first is that the questions and tasks students complete are calibrated to continually stretch their learning by moving forward once mastery has been achieved. The second is that the computer doesn't get tired, as a human might, in providing the more extensive practice a student might need before advancing to the next level. The third is that the computer has no views on whether the student is naughty or has some label, and the student can deliberately practice many times without the (often nonverbal) messages that they are slow, should have gotten it the first (few) times, and not seen to slow down the rest of the class.

That said, an intelligent tutoring system (ITS) such as ALEKS, Cognitive Tutor, and Operation ARIES is not plug-'n'-play. We don't sit students in front of a computer and hope for the best. Teachers should receive professional learning and have

MODULE 8

a plan for how ITS is used within the student's overall learning. As with adult tutoring, there should be clear outcomes and a referral process for use, as well as a plan to monitor progress and communicate with families. Researchers and developers of ITS are careful in reporting how they should be used, as they are not a substitute for instruction. An implementation danger is that a student who is already behind will be abandoned and left to languish on a computer program with little interface with an educator. One of the major advantages of ITS is that it provides valuable data for the teacher to use to plan instruction. However, in one study of ALEKS implementation, these data were not commonly used (Phillips et al., 2020). You'll recall similar cautions in the Module 7 discussion about online credit recovery courses, which currently are by and large not ITS but rather piles of independent work. Oversight by and interaction with a caring educator is crucial for a successful tutoring experience.

SUPPLEMENTATION INTERVENTION

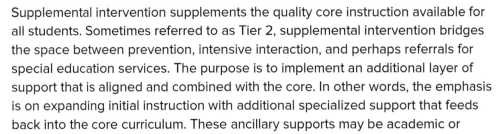

Supplemental intervention supplements the quality core instruction available for all students. Sometimes referred to as Tier 2, supplemental intervention bridges the space between prevention, intensive interaction, and perhaps referrals for special education services. The purpose is to implement an additional layer of support that is aligned and combined with the core. In other words, the emphasis is on expanding initial instruction with additional specialized support that feeds back into the core curriculum. These ancillary supports may be academic or behavioral, and above all, they are designed to accelerate the progress of students who are falling behind.

THE DELIVERY OF SUPPLEMENTAL INTERVENTION DOESN'T ALWAYS ENSURE THAT STUDENTS ARE INCREASINGLY SUCCESSFUL IN THE CORE CURRICULUM.

Evidence suggests that effective supplemental interventions include size, amount, frequency, and types of assessments. These teacher-directed small groups of two to five students meet a few times a week within the classroom. This is another argument for the importance of small group learning as part of the instructional design. In classrooms where small group instruction is the norm, meeting with a group for designated Tier 2 supplemental intervention is not disruptive. Student progress is monitored one to two times per month. Academic progress-monitoring tools include timed writing, vocabulary assessments, timed math exercises, and oral reading fluency. Social and emotional monitoring tools can include emotional check-ins, reflective discussions, and social skills ratings.

Unfortunately, the delivery of supplemental intervention doesn't always ensure that students are increasingly successful in the core curriculum. Instead, students are pulled away from quality core instruction in order to deliver some other instruction. Even worse, the content or skills being taught may have little to do with what is needed in the classroom. Rather than timely supports, they may be disconnected from the daily life of the student. It supplants, rather than supplements, what the student should be learning. The outcomes are disappointing to the student and the teacher, as the student sees that he is missing out on what is happening in the class, while the teacher wonders why he isn't generalizing concepts and skills. Schools with robust Tier 2 systems recognize that they must design and monitor their own efforts to ensure that the promise of supplemental instruction is realized.

Tier 2 supplemental instruction typically occurs within the flow of the classroom and is marked by its authentic and naturalistic responsiveness to student needs. These supplemental supports are delivered either prior to or after core instruction. For example, a student who needs social and emotional supports may meet with the teacher the day before a scheduled field trip so they can identify strategies he'll use during stressful moments. A small group of students may meet with the teacher after initial writing instruction to review and practice a new skill before applying it on their own.

Many of the problems associated with poorly implemented supplemental instruction can be prevented by developing a team approach to design, implementation, and monitoring of Tier 2 efforts. School teams should consist of general and special education teachers, specialists, and school leaders to ensure that the collective efficacy of the school continues to grow.

The questions in the following Pause and Ponder were designed to assist schools in refining existing systems of support. A current challenge is that Tier 2 systems have likely been in place for a decade or more and deserve to be revisited and strengthened. The task list leads school teams through a process that ensures that the goals of the school—to better support the academic and social and emotional needs of all students—are realized. Who might be recruited to strengthen your school's Tier 2 supplemental instruction efforts?

PAUSE & PONDER

In the second column, write the name(s) of the individual or team who will assume responsibility for the task identified in the first column. In the third column, write the deadline for or status of the task.

TASK	RESPONSIBLE INDIVIDUAL/TEAM	TIMELINE/STATUS
Identify structure or makeup of problem-solving team.		
Select resources, curricula, and interventions for use with standard protocol approach in reading (decoding and comprehension), math, and writing.		

(Continued)

(Continued)

TASK	RESPONSIBLE INDIVIDUAL/TEAM	TIMELINE/STATUS
Create and continue the development of resources on evidence-based instructional strategies to support identified students.		
Schedule time for general and special education teachers to collaborate, observe, implement, and evaluate strategies.		
Develop decision rules (cut scores, exit criteria) for remaining in or moving out of Tier 2 and beyond (responsiveness vs. unresponsiveness).		
Implement a system of data collection and progress monitoring for Tier 2 and beyond (see Section 2: Progress Monitoring for more information) to determine level and growth rate.		
Provide professional development opportunities for problem solving and protocol approaches.		
Ensure time is scheduled and process is established for teams to meet and review student needs.		
Determine level of intensity of instruction for Tier 2 and beyond (how often, how long, size of instructional group).		
Identify measures and procedures to document fidelity of implementation of interventions.		

Source: Johnson, E., Mellard, D. F., Fuchs, D., & McKnight, M. A. (2006). Responsiveness to intervention (RTI): How to do it. National Research Center on Learning Disabilities. https://files.eric.ed.gov/fulltext/ED496979.pdf.

REFLECT

Do you know what your students need to learn? Are you using the standards to identify concepts and skills that are critical in their progression of learning?

CASE IN POINT

Educators at Sycamore Middle School were dissatisfied with their Tier 2 supplemental instruction even before the pandemic. Learning walks conducted in late 2019 revealed that there was a range of supports being delivered. In some cases, they occurred in the classroom, but more often, they seemed to be accomplished through pullout programs that caused students to miss vital core instruction. Teachers had expressed frustration with interrupted instruction, students were anxious about missing important content, and it seemed like specialists and classroom teachers were operating in separate (and sometimes conflicting) lanes. When the school had to suddenly shift to distance learning in the spring of 2020, their attention necessarily turned to making online learning work. Now that Sycamore will be returning to in-person learning in the near future, they are determined to ensure that they don't make the same mistakes again.

School principal Althea Kingston created a task force of interested faculty, seeking in some cases to recruit key stakeholders. "I wanted to make sure we had a healthy representation of teachers who had been at Sycamore for a while, mixed in with those who are newer to our school," she said. Dr. Kingston explained that she wanted to be able to move beyond what had always been done in order to incorporate new perspectives. "In the meantime, I didn't want to

MODULE 8

lose the institutional knowledge of why we designed a Tier 2 system this way in the first place."

Their first order of business was to define and revisit why supplemental instruction is crucial. "You can't get to what needs to be done until you're clear on why it should be done," Dr. Jackson told the problem-solving team at their first meeting. By the end of the session, the team had outlined what was currently working and what wasn't. The team heard from members about the lack of clarity in terms of which students were targeted for supplemental instruction, how they were identified, and for how long. Several newer faculty members noted that no one had ever talked with them about professional learning for Tier 2 supports. "We just get a list of some general guidelines," one teacher noted. "I'm glad we're getting these out on the table," said Dr. Kingston. "Let's take a look at the task sheet and determine what we want to take on for our next meeting."

REFLECT

What would you suggest the team discuss at their next meeting? What advice might you offer to this group of educators?

INTENSIVE INTERVENTIONS

There are a smaller group of students in any school who require more intensive intervention to accelerate their progress. These students have experienced Tier 2 supplemental intervention, but their progress has been stalled, as evidenced by progress monitoring. These daily interventions are commonly delivered at the individual level, often by a specialist. Because of the nature of these intensive interventions, students may be receiving these supports outside of the classroom. The key to successful Tier 3 intensive interventions is having them tied as closely as possible to classroom content. This requires a higher level of communication between the classroom teacher and the specialist, especially in linking skills learned during intervention time with opportunities to practice them in the classroom.

Assignment of students to intensive interventions should be approached with caution, as the evidence of one-to-one instruction is mixed (Vaughn et al., 2007). In addition to the high cost to students in terms of missed instruction, there is a limit as to the capacity of a school to offer intensive interventions. Having said that, consider that intensive interventions should have a narrow focus so that students can make gains more quickly. Diagnostic assessments are utilized in order to identify high-leverage skills that will assist students in generalizing to wider knowledge. For instance, a student may benefit from an intensive intervention focused on phonics in order to spur gains in word recognition, fluency, and comprehension. A child who has difficulty with anger may be proactively taught several coping techniques to use in highly emotional situations. The goal of Tier 3 intensive interventions is not to address a broad list of skills (e.g., reading at grade level or exhibiting self-regulation skills) but rather to provide a narrow but deep dive into a skill that will shift the trajectory of a student's academic or social and emotional learning.

> THE KEY TO SUCCESSFUL TIER 3 INTENSIVE INTERVENTIONS IS HAVING THEM TIED AS CLOSELY AS POSSIBLE TO CLASSROOM CONTENT.

A barrier to effective Tier 3 intensive interventions concerns roles and responsibilities. In other words, it's the adults who can get in the way. This is usually motivated by all the right intentions—educators are consistent in their focus on students. But in doing so, they can overlook the needs of the adults who are also supporting them. And it is the student who suffers when we're not coordinating our efforts. What should be a system of supports can become a disjointed and confusing experience for them. After all, it isn't fair to have to rely on an eight-year-old to make sure the adults are on the same page. That is our responsibility.

Teachers can find intensive intervention to be particularly daunting in part because they may be more removed from the process. In particular, teacher recommendations for improving response to intervention processes include (Castro-Villarreal, Rodriguez, & Moore, 2014):

- Professional learning
- Time to collaborate
- Resources, especially human ones
- Communication with colleagues
- Streamlining processes to organize, simplify, and clarify all the moving parts

MODULE 8

With the exception of professional learning, all of these recommendations speak to the importance of how it is that we come together as a school community. A high degree of collective responsibility for all students in the school (not just the ones on your roster) is a mark of an effective school (Morales-Chicas & Agger, 2017). This should not be confused with everybody trying to do the same job— this is a case when redundancy is not a sign of a cohesive network. On the other hand, what happens more often is that unintended gaps occur when there are unstated assumptions about what others are doing. The following Pause and Ponder is a tool to use as a starting point for discussing roles and responsibilities. This should not be viewed as a rigid frame, as each school has its own unique strengths and context. But even the best-designed RTI system is going to get stale with each passing year. Revisit existing roles and responsibilities annually to ensure that a coordinated system is in place.

PAUSE & PONDER

Review the roles and responsibilities of response to intervention.

GENERAL EDUCATION[1]	SPECIALIST/SUPPORT STAFF[2]	ADMINISTRATION[3]
Implement Tier 1 level instruction with fidelity. Conduct progress monitoring of all students. Evaluate and identify students as at-risk and eligible for Tier 2 and beyond. Depending on protocol adopted by the school, provide Tier 2 and beyond interventions. Continue progress monitoring within Tier 1 of students in Tier 2 and beyond for comparison of growth with supplementary instruction and when supplementary instruction is discontinued.	Provide Tier 2 and beyond instruction to small groups. Monitor progress of students within Tier 2 and beyond and analyze results for the consideration of continuation of intervention, exit, or movement to increasingly intense levels of instruction. Collaborate with general education teacher to understand the Tier 1 instructional program and provide instructional/supplemental activities that can be embedded within Tier 1 to provide additional support to targeted students.	Provide resources for Tier 2 and beyond, including appropriate reading intervention program, trained staff, a system for progress monitoring in both Tier 1 and Tier 2 and beyond, and time for staff collaboration to make decisions about movement of students within the tiers. Lead the problem-solving model approach.

GENERAL EDUCATION[1]	SPECIALIST/SUPPORT STAFF[2]	ADMINISTRATION[3]
If another interventionist provides Tier 2 and beyond instruction, collaborate with that staff member on instructional methods used in Tier 1, monitoring progress and incorporating some of the intervention in the classroom to provide continued support for targeted students.	Promote a standard treatment protocol of problem-solving model consistently.	

1. *General education* includes the general education teacher.

2. *Specialist/support staff* includes the special education teacher, reading or learning specialists, related services personnel, paraprofessionals.

3. *Administration* includes building principals and assistants as well as curriculum or assessment specialists at building or district levels.

Source: Johnson, E., Mellard, D. F., Fuchs, D., & McKnight, M. A. (2006). *Responsiveness to intervention (RTI): How to do it.* National Research Center on Learning Disabilities. https://files.eric.ed.gov/fulltext/ED496979.pdf.

REFLECT

Who coordinates Tier 3 intensive intervention efforts at your school? What are the current strengths of your school's Tier 3 efforts? Where are their opportunities for growth?

Grasslands Elementary School has invested in social and emotional learning as a schoolwide focus for the past two years. Their work has produced noticeable results, as evidenced by increases in family involvement, student climate surveys, and teacher focus groups. "I've seen real improvements in the ways children talk to each other and work with each other," said assistant principal Trevor Williams.

Their previous work in this realm has led them to focus more intentionally on trauma-informed schooling. They know their community has been hit particularly hard by the pandemic. Staff at the school have engaged in professional learning and book studies to better understand both effects of trauma on students and signs that a child is currently suffering or has in the past. Using state grants, they have been able to hire a social worker and an additional counselor at the school last year to further support their Tier 3 intensive interventions for students who have experienced trauma. This has meant that students in need of individual therapeutic counseling are now able to access these supports. "We're a rural community, and services like this are usually in the city. The problem is, it's a seventy-mile round trip to get there," said Mr. Williams. "It's been a game changer to be able to do this here."

With new services, new problems can arise. Tier 3 social and emotional interventions have only been in place for a short time, while the academically oriented response to intervention process has been operating for a decade. Some of the traditional communication pathways the school has relied on for academic interventions don't work as well. "We've had access to a district reading specialist and a math specialist who are in the building twice a week. They work with a handful of teachers to do intensive interventions and meet each month with teacher teams," said Mr. Williams. "But we don't have that in place on the SEL side." The social worker and the new counselor have not had a lot of experience in working with other educators. They have expressed concern about issues of confidentiality in discussing what they have been doing with identified students, so they have erred on the side of caution. Classroom teachers tell him they would like to support these efforts in their classrooms but really don't have a sense of what goes on or what the outcomes should be.

REFLECT

Mr. Williams wants to do some fact-gathering before he forms a team to improve alignment between Tier 3 intensive interventions and the schoolwide SEL and trauma-informed efforts. What three to five questions do you advise him to investigate? What advice do you have for him about potential pitfalls?

QUESTIONS TO LEARN MORE	PITFALLS TO AVOID
•	•
•	•
•	•
•	•
•	•

SPRING FORWARD

The concept of intervention has existed in education for many decades. Some schools appear to implement these systems well; others not so much. If there ever were a time to ensure that students who needed intervention received those services, it's now. The key is to identify the right students—the ones who really need the interventions. If you see the news feeds, it appears that all of our students need intensive intervention. We encourage you to take a step back and review the screening data. What does that information tell you? Create a system to monitor students' progress throughout the year so you know if there are times that other students need intervention services. And, as we have noted before, don't spend all of your energy focused on the gaps and deficits. Rather, think about all of the things you can do to help students take giant leaps in their learning. Remember, their technology skills have likely grown a lot in the past year, so don't forget to use that resource in your efforts.

REFLECT

Reflect on your learning about learning leaps and intervention efforts. Identify actions you are considering based on your learning.

IMPORTANT

On a scale of 1 to 5, with 5 being very important and 1 being not important at all, how would you rate the value of learning leaps and intervention efforts in your classroom or school?

1   2   3   4   5

WAIT, BUT WHY?

Explain your reason for the rating above.

A CALL TO ACTION: RETHINKING SCHOOL

In 2020, we added a new chapter to the history of schooling—the world shut down schooling as we knew it, and teachers and school leaders adapted to many new technologies. In our lives and in those around us, we experienced much angst caused by sickness, uncertainty, social isolation, and fewer opportunities for employment. Many have rushed to proclaim gloom and doom in education and have been blind to the many positives that have occurred. It will be some time before the research is compiled as to what worked well, for whom, and when, and what did not. It is likely to be a broadsheet of mixed messages, but one conclusion is obvious—we were given the opportunity to disrupt the usual grammar of schooling and to explore new options.

The greatest travesty that can arise for schools is if we rush back to the old normal and learn nothing, or little, about what worked well. That's why this book has focused on rebounding and taking the opportunity to create an even better schooling system, one that serves even more students and focuses more on what matters most. Rebounding involves bouncing back, getting better (e.g., "His learning is on the rebound."), and capitalizing on an opportunity—and we conclude this book by highlighting major learnings from the events of 2020.

The claims throughout these modules are based on early research, our lived experiences, and listening to the experiences of students and teachers in our school community and via many social media resources. Our aim is to capitalize on the more positive experiences and invite educators to bring back these experiences as part of the next normal in our schools. We begin by **resolving** to reduce that which we were doing that was not so effective and add new ideas to bring back better. We acknowledge our **relief and resilience** as we face challenges and work out mitigation strategies to enhance the learning lives of our students.

> THE GREATEST TRAVESTY THAT CAN ARISE FOR SCHOOLS IS IF WE RUSH BACK TO THE OLD NORMAL AND LEARN NOTHING, OR LITTLE, ABOUT WHAT WORKED WELL.

We know that it would be so much easier to **return and re-open** and rush back to the old ways of teaching and learning. There is comfort in this old normality; students and teachers know their roles and hierarchies, and it has worked for many decades. But we also know that only about 4 of 10 students by the end of elementary school want to come to school to learn (Jenkins, 2016), that too many students strive to leave school as soon as they are allowed, and that we have created an industry of labeling to find ways to explain why so many students fail to thrive in schooling. The old is not necessarily comforting or of high value to these students. Not that they necessarily have done better during the pandemic, but we recognize we have been given an opportunity to reflect on how to make schooling more enticing, effective, and efficient for more of our students—that is the invitation that **rebound** offers us.

So, we ask you to **reimagine** the ways in which learning can occur and have placed a premium on teaching the skills of self-regulation or learning agency. Among the most impacted were those students who most depended on teachers, and where teachers overorchestrated their classrooms and the learning. The least impacted were primarily those (students and teachers) who had the skills of self-regulation as they were more likely to know how to choose strategies for learning, seek and act on feedback, and monitor their progress.

THERE IS PROBABLY NOT A PARENT, POLITICIAN, OR POLICY PUNDIT WHO DID NOT SEE AND RECOGNIZE THE SKILLS OF EDUCATORS DURING THIS TIME.

So how can we **redefine and reinvent** and do this collectively so that educators lead the revolution to build schools where learning is fun, efficient, effective, and visible to all? The pandemic has provided a fast-track opportunity for the profession to regroup, restructure schooling, and to ask, *What are the optimal processes to use to run our schools and classes?* This book invites more of this debate. While it is certainly the case that many students, teachers, and schools already emphasized teaching the skills of self-regulation and high agency, where learning in all its messiness was the norm, and where it was okay to *not know* and to enjoy the thrill of discovery, now is the time to build on our discoveries such as the positive focus on self-regulation, and create a new and better grammar of schooling. As we said in the introduction, "If we want to survive and thrive, we need to rebound from these experiences. We need to redefine and reinvent. The time is now. The opportunity is ours."

ESTEEMING TEACHER EXPERTISE

During the pandemic, we have seen the expertise of educators dominate. There is probably not a parent, politician, or policy pundit who did not see and recognize the skills of educators during this time. Unlike parents with one to three children in the home class, teachers have twenty to thirty at once and can motivate them to engage in activities that the students initially do not know how to do. Teachers know how to make the struggle of learning joyful and can provide feedback at the right time and in the right way to each student. Teachers do not permit children to continually ask, "Is this right?" and teachers do not "do" the work for their students. Teachers know where to go next for each student's learning, how to balance the breadth and depth of the ever-varied school curriculum, and invest in after-school work of marking, preparing, developing resources, and going to professional learning and meetings. And teachers do all this for 200+ days a year for at least five hours every day.

This is a time to identify, esteem, privilege, and appreciate the expertise of educators. This expertise is very much a function of how educators think and make decisions and judgments. Their deep knowledge and core skills have a major impact on the learning lives of students. Rickards et al. (2020) identified evaluative thinking as the key to the profession of teaching and leading schools. They outlined six key educative questions underpinned by evaluative thinking:

1. What is the student ready to learn, and what evidence supports this?

2. What are the possible and preferred evidence-based interventions?

3. What is the expected impact on learning and how will this be evaluated?

4. How will the preferred intervention be resourced and implemented?

5. What happened and how can this be interpreted?

6. How do I collaborate with others (e.g., colleagues, students, research) to gain insight into my impact?

They then outlined at least five ways of thinking evaluatively:

1. Reasoning and critical thinking about evidence leading to "where to next" recommendations

2. Addressing the fidelity of implementation, continually checking for unintended consequences, and allowing for adaptations to maximize the value of outcomes and experiences for students

3. Investigating potential biases and confounding factors that may lead to false conclusions or decisions

4. Appreciating that the primary aim of teaching is to have a desirable, significant, and worthwhile impact on students

5. Understanding others' points of view, leading to judgments of value or worth. This evaluative thinking (the questions and ways of thinking) was and still remains paramount.

NEVER SAY EDUCATORS CAN'T CHANGE, ADAPT, OR SHOW RESILIENCE.

Throughout the pandemic, many schools ran hybrid and simultaneous systems, which included teachers teaching some students in front of them at school while simultaneously working with students at home via the internet. They also participated in professional learning on how to use the district's required learning management systems and the technology that enabled them to teach remote students—without a grumble, but with a plan and a positive disposition. It is hard to locate a single policy or government edict (other than whether schools should open or not) that provided information about how to teach during these times. It was left to schools. And that they adapted, changed, worried about what was optimal for their students, and created solutions is remarkable. Never say educators can't change, adapt, or show resilience. We need to consider ways to recognize and harness this expertise at adaptation and change in future discussions about school policies. This was and still is truly an educator-led revolution.

LEARNING HOW TO LEARN

A major theme throughout this playbook is teaching the skills of learning agency and self-regulation—that is, knowing when to apply various strategies; knowing when and how to avoid distractions; knowing about one's own thinking skills; knowing learning strategies and whether they are working and, if not, changing them; and knowing how to self-evaluate. When students leave our school, self-regulation becomes among the most critical skills—when they attend university, on the job, and in out-of-school activities. When the teacher is not present, self-regulation takes over, and a key regulation skill is knowing how and when to seek the help of others, such as teachers.

THE MOST CRITICAL TASK IN THE REBOUND PROCESS IS EXCELLENT DIAGNOSES.

The intent is to deliberately teach all students these skills. They can be taught, and their absence was sorely noted by teachers, parents, and students during online learning. The low-regulation students were overreliant on structure, demanded crystal-clear directions, and sought lots of feedback that they were right or at least *doing* the right stuff. Higher-regulation students were more adept at working through messy structures, working out what the directions really meant, and were able to seek and use feedback about their progress, where to go next, and what to revisit. Students in schools that already taught these skills had far fewer hassles, and indeed many thrived during this time. So we all need to teach in a way that develops these skills, ensure the mantra is "'gradual release of responsibility," and see self-regulation as a critical outcome of our teaching.

DIAGNOSE AND SUPPORT

The most critical task in the rebound process is excellent diagnoses. Which students thrived; which did not? Yes, the media and many academic blogs are full of angst that the "usual" disadvantaged groups need to be catered to—and yes, they do—but we should take care to not confuse categories of students (such as those from low socioeconomic families, English learners, students with autism, etc.) with individual students. Some of these students have done very well at home, and some not. As part of diagnoses, consider the following questions:

1. Which students struggle with low self-regulation to maintain learning progression, that is, those who are highly dependent on the teacher?

2. Which students return with high levels of stress and social and emotional concerns with possible behavioral issues arising? Galton, Morrison, and Pell (2000) showed that the greatest predictor of success when students move schools (or, in pandemic times, move from in-home learning back to in-school learning) is whether they make a friend in the first month. Be attentive to who is or is not rebuilding friendships. School is not much without friends.

3. Which students have no or low proficiency in using quality learning strategies?

4. Which students have had access to fewer educational resources and activities relative to their peers due to limited digital engagement? (This includes the percentage who did not log on at all during the homeschooling!)

5. Which students had a lack of progress in school prior to at-home teaching?

6. Which students had low concepts of themselves as a learner at school or at home, and even more so on return?

7. Which students are living in homes that are not safe havens (for many of these students, school is the safe haven), such that learning from home might cause an exacerbation of physical and emotional health issues?

8. Which students have parents who have low capacity or desire to engage them in the schoolwork at home and who ignore or permit no engagement with schoolwork?

THE RESEARCH EVIDENCE

There are numerous reports bewailing the predicted loss of learning as a result of the education structures in place during the pandemic, but most assume students received no or very little teaching during pandemic times, and they underestimate teachers' skill at rebounding and rebooting. The assumption often seems to be that "reduced" contact by not being in school is necessarily negative. Counting the hours and days spent in front of teachers is a poor predictor of much—if it were the case, Australian students would be top of the world and Finnish near the bottom (as the former has among the longest school hours and days per year and the latter among the fewest). One of the powerful words to emerge from this time, alongside effectiveness, is *efficiency*. Many students are asking why is it they can complete the work in much less time without the distraction of the whole class, without teachers setting time limits (which can be too long), and ask, "What did I use to do all day in school?" We need to appreciate that students have differential efficiencies as they complete their work and build that into the new school day.

COUNTING THE HOURS AND DAYS SPENT IN FRONT OF TEACHERS IS A POOR PREDICTOR OF MUCH.

Other reports are taking small differences and magnifying the implications. For example, Engzell, Frey, and Verhagen (2020) released a report based on 350,000 students in Netherland schools. The headlines were sensational—the authors blogged that the learning loss from the pandemic was "worse than you think." Despite the Netherlands having a strong infrastructure (e.g., more than 90% enjoyed broadband even among the poorest quartile of households), their study found

> robust evidence that students are still learning less in lockdown than in a normal year. The lost progress amounts to about a fifth of a school year, almost exactly the same period that schools remained closed (assuming a regular school year is ten months). In other words, the data suggest that nearly every hour out of school was an hour of lost student learning.

The effect size across math, reading, and spelling was −0.08, which, relative to the many influences in schooling, is quite small. A good, robust program is most likely to recover this learning quite rapidly.

In the southern hemisphere, COVID hit first near the start of the academic year, so there have been eight months of experiences to understand the impact of out-of-class teaching. Victoria, Australia, for example, had over five months of at-home teaching, mostly with major lockdown rules that severely restricted movement. We know a lot about what worked and what did not work—primarily based on surveys from 60 schools, 14,000+ parents, 20,000 students, weekly school leader surveys, 28 workshops and focus groups, and the usual department data sets (e.g., about absenteeism, well-being) (State of Victoria, 2020; see also AHISA study, 2020).

Some findings include

- School attendance rates remained high; the vast majority of students took part in remote and flexible learning every day.

- Morale also stayed high, in the main, as teachers and school leaders worked together to address difficult dilemmas with a sense of mutual respect and common purpose.

- Parents gained unprecedented insight into their children's education and school.

- Students mostly highly rated COVID teaching and they liked the freedom and flexibilities to work at their own pace and to their own schedule, the comfort of home, no travel to and from school, more time for nonschool activities, less stress, and fewer distractions.

- New skills have been acquired; new pedagogical opportunities trialed.

And yes, there were challenges. There was the sadness of illness, death, and economic hardships; there were reduced physical friendship groups; and there were many students who lacked supportive family environments to access learning or even log on to classes. About 10 percent of students from disadvantaged schools were absent during the remote learning period, compared to about 4 percent of students from advantaged schools—reflecting what also happens when in class. A surprising outcome was that many students who are normally shy and quiet in class spoke up and contributed more to the online environment; some "naughty" students were less distracted at home; there were many teachers and school leaders who reported that many students were more engaged with online learning. Nevertheless, more than one in eight students found it hard to maintain focus and not get distracted at home. Would you welcome only one in eight being distracted in the regular class?

The major findings included the following:

1. **Better connections with parents.** School principals, teachers, and parents all spoke overwhelmingly of the positive relationships built over the period of remote and flexible learning. Many parents sat alongside their children during this period, and they have become more engaged in their children's learning and now better understand their work. Schools also learned more about the home situations of some vulnerable students and could better incorporate these insights into their teaching and student support. Maybe we need to rethink the usual "student reports" we labor over and send home once or twice a year (on the basis of analyzing these reports, Hattie and Peddie [2003] found that 98 percent of children are achieving well, putting in the effort, and a pleasure to teach. Such public relation lies are indefensible and a waste of teachers creative writing skills and time) and instead use social media to organize student-led conferences, involve parents with their students in teach-back sessions more often, and keep the focus on helping parents learn the language of learning that they saw so vividly during COVID teaching.

2. **Greater flexibility of remote learning.** There is much evidence from numerous school leaders and teachers that many students enjoyed, and some students excelled in, exercising greater student agency with the flexibility that came with remote learning. This did not happen by assigning work to students and leaving them alone—that was tried and failed (not surprisingly). Teachers had to use learner- and backward-design to structure classes, to teach more self-regulation, to implement a greater and faster release of responsibility by the teacher, to teach students how to work with others, and to have many formative evaluative opportunities to check and diagnose progress. Yes, many struggled with traditional testing, realizing that more transparency of what success means and looks like and more diagnostic assessment (particularly by listening to students thinking and voice, and as outlined in this book) was much more appropriate and informative. They found technological tools to allow students to showcase their understanding in exciting ways.

> SCHOOL PRINCIPALS, TEACHERS, AND PARENTS SPOKE OVERWHELMINGLY OF THE POSITIVE RELATIONSHIPS BUILT OVER REMOTE AND FLEXIBLE LEARNING.

3. **Expanding online learning.** A number of schools emphasized the benefits of putting lessons and teaching videos online for students to access whenever they wanted. Numerous teachers spoke of how they have used technology to provide more engaging resources for students. Teachers also saw value in being able to talk to students online at times convenient to both parties. And students could view recorded

lessons as many times as they wished without having to acknowledge that they were doing this (and appearing not smart in front of peers and teachers). Many high school students will be much more prepared for college and university, as they have been working with video and online classes for some time and are far less teacher directive than high schools.

4. **Students with special needs.** The experiences of remote and flexible learning for these students were as varied as the students themselves. Beware of generalizations. Maybe now is the time to *stop* categorizing students and see them all as learners. Yes, funding follows labels, but it has major downsides assuming all students with the same label should have the same accommodations and differential teaching. The effect size of the achievement of two similar students—one labeled and one not—is −0.60: devastating to the student when false expectations are foisted on them. The alternative is to consider "learning interventions" the right of every student; the role of teachers is to develop optimal learning interventions focusing on what the student brings to the lesson, evaluating the impact of interventions to see the effects on the student learning, and ensuring all students attain the success criteria as outlined in curricula statements. Across Victoria, many of these students in COVID teaching enjoyed the experience, thrived on the absence of peer interruption, and enjoyed greater flexibility and choice in the timing, sequence, and depth of their learning. Attendance increased for many of these students relative to the same time in the previous school year.

5. **Increasing the effectiveness and efficiency of how schools operate.** During COVID teaching, school meetings were minimized, there was increased cooperation among teachers, and in many schools, we truly saw distributed leadership and the development of collective teacher efficacy in action. Teachers spoke glowingly of the efforts and effective leadership of many school leaders.

Webber (2020) used New Zealand assessment data from 500,000+ students over a ten-year period to compare COVID to pre-COVID experiences. He found that scores in reading and mathematics were slightly higher during COVID teaching than what the model predicts based on historical patterns, there was no evidence for a substantial loss of learning in these subjects, but results were more concerning for writing. As we noted, attention to the skills of writing is likely to be most worthwhile in any reboot program.

Kuhfeld and colleagues (2020a) used NWEA's extensive database of 4.4 million third through eighth grade U.S. students who completed a test in 2020 compared to 2019. They found that students performed similarly in reading to same-grade students in fall 2019, but about 5 to 10 percentile points lower in math. The picture that is emerging from these studies suggests that each school should have a bold program in place of diagnosing the achievement and social and emotional learning of each and all returning students and, as noted above, not make assumptions based on prior classifications of students.

In her survey of New Zealand teachers, Hood (2020) reported that it was the same factors in class and at home that made the most positive impact, such as "balancing attention to student well-being and relationships with academic learning, high expectations that are clearly communicated and upheld, rigorous learning tasks that activate hard thinking and deep learning, instructional practices informed by the science of learning, regular and clear feedback, and a balance between flexibility and routine" (p. 4). For the students, "the key was whether students held the requisite competencies and knowledge to engage in the more independent style of learning that was required of them during the lockdown period [and these] also impacted engagement and learning outcomes" (p. 5). Parents argued that learning at home was most successful when there was consistency across a whole school and among classes. For teachers, the lockdown period was an opportunity for considerable professional learning and growth, prompting the development of new skills and knowledge, as well as new opportunities for teacher collaboration and cooperation.

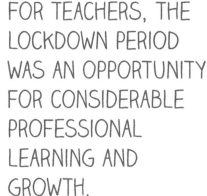

FOR TEACHERS, THE LOCKDOWN PERIOD WAS AN OPPORTUNITY FOR CONSIDERABLE PROFESSIONAL LEARNING AND GROWTH.

Echoing the claims throughout this book, Hood argued that three major teaching practices mattered most, both in class and at home:

1. Maintaining high expectations and holding students accountable for meeting these expectations was critical for maintaining students' motivation and engagement and facilitating learning.

2. Utilizing a variety of tasks that were well-matched to the intended learning outcomes and moving beyond low-level tasks and "busy work" to engage students in meaningful learning, supported motivation, and engagement.

3. Establishing some form of routine or daily structure provided a greater likelihood that students would stay up to date with work and maintain engagement.

When teaching online, teachers may have needed to implement more regular formative evaluation and give more feedback connected to the expectations set by the teacher, as this was seen as crucial for motivation and engagement as well as for ongoing learning. This also entailed structuring activities and teaching students so that they were more able to manage their time, prioritize activities, and select suitable strategies and overcome challenges (the very essence of self-regulation). What was lost during at-home teaching was the social component of learning, greater engagement with friends and the social aspect of schooling, and shared student experiences. There were fewer spontaneous teaching and teachable moments—those opportunities that arise in the natural flow of a class to dig deeper into an idea, to explore a new idea in greater detail, or to demonstrate the connection between ideas.

Kraft and Falken (2021) surveyed about 8,000 teachers across nine U.S. states about the challenges they faced during COVID teaching compared to pre-COVID. They all "struggled" to engage their students in learning, with having their own children at home, and the more veteran teachers reported concerns with learning and adapting to teaching via technology. Teachers working in high-poverty schools and in schools that serve a majority of Black students reported a "precipitous drop in their self-reported sense of success," with 53 percent of teachers reporting a decline in their sense of success teaching online compared to in-class teaching. However, they found that teachers who had strong communication among colleagues, fair expectations, and a recognition of effort from the top, along with targeted professional development and facilitated, meaningful collaboration with colleagues, were least likely to experience a dip in their sense of success.

Reimers and Schleicher (2020) surveyed 1,370 educators across 59 countries and started their report by noting the "remarkable resilience, flexibility and commitment to education in having established strategies for education continuity, in extremely challenging conditions, during the COVID-19 pandemic" (p. 3). What is fascinating is that 70 percent claimed that the strategies put into place for COVID teaching were well planned and well executed, and most claimed that the plans were NOT designed top-down but by those closer to the students in a collaborative manner among teachers and school leaders—confirming the educator-led revolution.

RECOMMENDATIONS FOR REBOOTING

There have been many reports with recommendations for how to reboot our schooling system after students return to regular schooling. Darling-Hammond, Schachner, and Edgerton (2020), for example, recommend (like we do) continuing to include online teaching as part of the next normal and encourage sharing pioneering efforts among districts, giving special consideration to early childhood learning; developing standards for digital learning that articulate how technology should be used to empower learners; enacting distance learning with attention to equity; shifting from measuring seat time to learning engagement; prioritizing assessments that illuminate student growth and learning; supporting acceleration of learning, not remediation; building capacity for inclusivity; and identifying safe, culturally responsive practice.

Our message is that we can learn from pandemic teaching and introduce many of the successful innovations back into in-class schooling. The old grammar of schooling—where teachers asked questions that required a less-than-three-word student response, where teachers did 90 percent of the talking, and where assessment and feedback were about the facts—needs to be replaced. The new syntax of learning invites students to talk about their thinking, not just report someone else's thinking, in classes where there is a balance of open and closed questions and tasks and where students elaborate, evaluate, rephrase, reason, and are challenged; where teachers work together to evaluate their impact—about what, for whom, and how much; where we allow students multiple pathways to success with differential time and involvement by teachers; and where we teach students the skills of learning agency so that they learn to become their own teachers. This is the essence of Visible Learning (https://us.corwin.com/en-us/nam/visible-learning).

In this new grammar of learning, teachers move (as they needed to do in online teaching) from talking, facts, and directing to triage: to listening to how students are thinking, seeing struggle as desirable, prioritizing next learning steps, focusing on the centrality of each student, enabling students to work and learn with other peers, and teaching them the skills of self-regulation. The technology revolution that has been coming for the past fifty years is now in full bloom. The greatest learning about how to use technology relates to the power of social media to transform talking to triage, transform talking to learning, and transform talking to hearing how students are thinking.

The power of social media has opened a new vista of possibilities. We know that learning is enhanced to the degree that errors and misunderstandings are diagnosed and identified, and errors are seen as opportunities. Social media is a powerful way to explore what we do not know—the pandemic exposed this head on—and this has empowered so many students to "talk" about how they are thinking, exposing the learning strategies that they are using during problem solving and doing. They are much more willing to type, video, and talk over social media about their "struggles" in learning—which is the very essence of learning. Children do not come to school to learn that which they already know but quickly learn that if they do not "know," they are graded, labeled, silenced. Failure must be a learner's best friend, and their use of social media opens up new vistas to privilege not knowing, encouraging them to question and query, and reintroducing the curiosity, discovery, and the power of "Why." These methods can be used when students return to in-class teaching: There is no need to retreat back to the old grammar of schooling.

THE TECHNOLOGY REVOLUTION THAT HAS BEEN COMING FOR THE PAST FIFTY YEARS IS NOW IN FULL BLOOM.

If we take this opportunity to really learn from what is happening during COVID teaching, we can reboot to more effective schooling for more students. But this will take superb leadership. Leaders who have demonstrated remarkable powers of resilience, ingenuity, listening, and empathy during these school disruptions need to also show these powers on the return to in-class learning and not hurry back to the comforts and familiarity of the old grammar of schooling.

The greatest power of a school leader is the major influence they have over the narrative in the school; make the narrative about professional learning from what has worked so well in pandemic teaching to meld with the old to create a new syntax around learning. Leaders also need to create the imperative and time for this to happen and work together to decide what to drop from the old grammar of schooling.

BOUNCING BACK

We know from past disruptions such as earthquakes, floods, strikes, and wars that we sadly learn little as we rush back to the comfort of our current schooling hierarchies: where the past winners want to go back to being winners again, where we blame and name kids who cannot learn, where we fight about autonomy and money, where we prefer and enjoy tweaking curricula, playing Olympic games via testing, and restrain rather than unleash the powerful profession of educators based on expertise and evaluative thinking. This pandemic may lead to a revolution in schooling, provided we take the opportunity to rebound: bounce back, bring back better, and capitalize on the opportunity.

Ainsworth, L. (2013). *Prioritizing the Common Core: Identifying specific standards to emphasize the most.* Corwin.

Almarode, J., Fisher, D., Thunder, K., & Frey, N. (2021). *The success criteria playbook: A hands-on guide to making learning visible and measurable.* Corwin.

American Psychological Association. (2017). *How do I know if I need therapy? PTSD Clinical Practice Guideline.* https://www.apa.org/ptsd-guideline/patients-and-families/seeking-therapy.pdf

American Psychological Association. (2018). *Stress effects on the body.* https://www.apa.org/topics/stress-body#:~:text=Chronic%20stress%2C%20or%20a%20constant,a%20toll%20on%20the%20body

Assessment Network. (2019). *Overcoming assessment bias: Making assessment fair for all learners.* https://www.assessmentnetwork.net/2019/02/overcoming-assessment-bias-making-assessment-fair-for-all-learners/

Association of Heads of Independent Schools of Australia (AHISA). (2020). *AHISA member schools: 2020 parents, students, and staff home-based learning detailed report.* Canberra, Australia: MMG Education.

Balfanz, R., & Byrnes, V. (2012). *The importance of being there: A report on absenteeism in the nation's public schools.* Johns Hopkins University Center for Social Organization of Schools.

Bandura, A. (1982). Self-efficacy mechanism in human agency. *American Psychologist, 37*(2), 122–147.

Bermejo-Toro, L., Prieto-Ursúa, M., & Hernández, V. (2016). Towards a model of teacher well-being: Personal and job resources involved in teacher burnout and engagement. *Educational Psychology, 36*(3), 481–501.

Berry, A. (2020). Disrupting to driving: Exploring upper primary teachers' perspectives on student engagement. *Teachers and Teaching, 26*(2), 145–165. https://doi.org/10.1080/13540602.2020.1757421

Boud, D. (2010). *Assessment 2020: Seven propositions for assessment reform in higher education.* Australian Learning and Teaching Council.

Brabeck, M., Jeffrey, J., & Fry, S. (2010). *Practice for knowledge acquisition (not drill and kill): Designing activities with the goal of transferring knowledge.* American Psychological Association. https://www.apa.org/education/k12/practice-acquisition

Brown, J. S., Collins, A., & Duguid, P. (1989). Situated cognition and the culture of learning. *Educational Researcher, 18*(1), 32–41.

California Association of School Counselors. (n.d.). *Connecting the dots: The school counselor role in student mental health.* https://ocde.us/MTSS/Documents/Connecting%20the%20Dots%20-%20School%20Counselors%20and%20Mental%20Health%206-5-20.pdf

Campitelli, G., & Gobet, F. (2011). Deliberate practice: Necessary but not sufficient. *Current Directions in Psychological Science, 20*(5), 280–285.

CASEL. (2020). *The CASEL guide to schoolwide SEL essentials.* https://schoolguide.casel.org/resource/the-casel-guide-to-schoolwide-sel-essentials

Castro-Villarreal, F., Rodriguez, B. J., & Moore, S. (2014, May). Teachers' perceptions and attitudes about Response to Intervention (RTI) in their schools: A qualitative analysis. *Teaching and Teacher Education, 40*, 104–112.

Collaborative for Academic, Social, and Emotional Learning (CASEL). (2020). *The CASEL guide to schoolwide SEL essentials.* https://schoolguide.casel.org/resource/the-casel-guide-to-schoolwide-sel-essentials/

Collins, A., Brown, J. S., & Newman, S. E. (1988). Cognitive apprenticeship. *Thinking: The Journal of Philosophy for Children, 8*(1), 2–10.

Colorado Department of Education. (2020). *Special education and COVID-19 FAQs.* https://www.cde.state.co.us/cdesped/special_education_faqs#:~:text= Compensatory%20educational%20services%20should%20be,the%20inability%20 to%20provide%20FAPE

Committee for Children. (2020, October 14). *Second Step middle school: Empowered with skills for life.* https://www.secondstep.org/middle-school-curriculum

Darling-Aduana, J., Good, A. G., & Heinrich, C. (2019). Mapping the inequity implications of help-seeking in high school online credit-recovery classrooms. *Teachers College Record, 121*(11), 1–17.

Darling-Hammond, L., Schachner, A., & Edgerton, A. K. (2020). *Restarting and reinventing school: Learning in the time of COVID and beyond.* https://learningpolicyinstitute .org/sites/default/files/product-files/Restart_Reinvent_Schools_COVID_REPORT.pdf

Davis, M. H., Mac Iver, M. A., Balfanz, R. W., Stein, M. L., & Fox, J. H. (2019). Implementation of an early warning indicator and intervention system. *Preventing School Failure, 63*(1), 77–88.

Deans for Impact. (2016). *Practice with purpose: The emerging science of teacher expertise.* https://deansforimpact.org/resources/practice-with-purpose

Deno, S. (1987, Fall). Curriculum-based measurement. *Teaching Exceptional Children,* 41–47.

Elbaum, B., Vaughn, S., Hughes, M. T., & Watson Moody, S. (2000). How effective are one-to-one tutoring programs in reading for elementary students at risk for reading failure? A meta-analysis of the intervention research. *Journal of Educational Psychology, 92*(4), 605–619. https://doi.org/10.1037/0022-0663.92.4.605

Elmer, J. (2019). Not sure what to say to someone with depression? Here are seven ways to show support. *Healthline.* https://www.healthline.com/health/what-to-say-to-someone-with-depression

Engzell, P., Frey, A., & Verhagen, M. (2020, November 9). *The collateral damage to children's education during lockdown.* https://voxeu.org/article/collateral-damage-children-s-education-during-lockdown

Ericsson, K. A., Krampe, R. T., & Tesch-Romer, C. (1993). The role of deliberate practice in the acquisition of expert performance. *Psychological Review, 100*(3), 363–406.

Essary, J. N., Barza, L., & Thurston, R. J. (2020). Secondary traumatic stress among educators. *Kappa Delta Pi Record, 56*(3), 116–121. https://doi.org/10.1080/00228958 .2020.1770004

Ewing, J. (2020, December 28). The ridiculousness of learning loss. *Forbes.* https:// www.forbes.com/sites/johnewing/2021/12/28/the-ridiculousness-of-learning-loss/?sh=45806f3b7c32

Filippello, P., Buzzai, C., Costa, S., Orecchio, S., & Sorrenti, L. (2020). Teaching style and academic achievement: The mediating role of learned helplessness and mastery orientation. *Psychology in the Schools, 57*(1), 5–16. https://doi.org/10.1002/pits.22315

Fisher, D. (2009). The use of instructional time in the typical high school classroom. *The Educational Forum, 73*, 168–176.

Fisher, D., & Frey, N. (2020). No instructional minute wasted. *Educational Leadership, 77*(9), 56–60.

Fisher, D., & Frey, N. (2021). *Better learning through structured teaching: A framework for the gradual release of responsibility* (3rd ed.). ASCD.

Fisher, D., Frey, N., Almarode, J., Flories, K., & Nagel, D. (2020a). *PLC+: Better decisions and greater impact by design*. Corwin.

Fisher, D., Frey, N., Almarode, J., Flories, K., & Nagel, D. (2020b). *The PLC+ playbook: A hands-on guide to collectively improving student learning grades K–12*. Corwin.

Fisher, D., Frey, N., Amador, O., & Assof, J. (2019). *The teacher clarity playbook: A hands-on guide to creating learning intentions and success criteria for organized, effective instruction*. Corwin.

Fisher, D., Frey, N., Bustamante, V., & Hattie, J. (2021). *The assessment playbook for distance and blended learning*. Corwin.

Fisher, D., Frey, N., & Hattie, J. (2020). *The distance learning playbook: Teaching for engagement and impact in any setting*. Corwin.

Fisher, D., Frey, N., Law, N., & Smith, D. (2020). *On-your-feet guide: Distance learning for instructional leaders*. Corwin.

Forlin, C., Hattie, J., & Douglas, G. (1996). Inclusion: Is it stressful for teachers? *Journal of Intellectual and Developmental Disability, 21*, 199–217.

Frey, N., & Fisher, D. (2013). A formative assessment system for writing improvement. *English Journal, 103*(1), 66–71.

Frey, N., Hattie, J., & Fisher, D. (2018). *Developing assessment-capable visible learners, grades K–12*. Corwin.

Fuchs, L. S., & Fuchs, D. (2006). Implementing responsiveness-to-intervention to identify learning disabilities. *Perspectives on Dyslexia, 32*(1), 39–43.

Galton, M., Morrison, I., & Pell, T. (2000). Transfer and transition in English schools: Reviewing the evidence. *International Journal of Educational Research, 33*(4), 341–363.

Garrett, R., & Hong, G. (2016). Impacts of grouping and time on the math learning of language minority kindergartners. *Educational Evaluation and Policy Analysis, 38*. https://doi.org/10.3102/0162373715611484

Gottfried, M. A. (2014). The influence of tardy classmates on students' socio-emotional outcomes. *Teachers College Record, 116*(3), 1–35.

Gottfried, M. A. (2019). Chronic absenteeism in the classroom context: Effects on achievement. *Urban Education, 54*(1), 3–34.

Greenstein, L. (2019, February 19). *Overcoming assessment bias: Making assessment fair for all learners*. https://www.assessmentnetwork.net/2019/02/overcoming-assessment-bias-making-assessment-fair-for-all-learners

Guessoum, S. B., Lachal, J., Radjak, R., Carretier, E., Minassian, S., Benoit, L., & Moro, M. R. (2020). Adolescent psychiatric disorders during COVID-19 pandemic and lockdown. *Psychiatry Research, 291*, 113264.

Hall, R. M., & Sandler, B. R. (1982). *The classroom climate: A chilly one for women?* https://files.eric.ed.gov/fulltext/ED215628.pdf

Hargraves, V. (2018). How to develop high expectation teaching. *The Education Hub*. https://theeducationhub.org.nz/how-to-develop-high-expectations-teaching.

Hargreaves, A., & Fullan, M. (2012). *Professional capital: Transforming teaching in every school*. Teachers College Press.

Hattie, J. (n.d.). *Global research database*. Visible Learning Meta[x]. https://www.visiblelearningmetax.com/Influences

Hattie, J., & Peddie, R. (2003). School *reports: "Praising with faint damns."* https://doi.org/10.18296/set.0710

Hattie, J., & Timperley, H. (2007). The power of feedback. *Review of Educational Research, 77*(1), 81–112.

Haydon, T., Marsicano, R., & Scott, T. (2013). A comparison of choral and individual responding: A review of the literature. *Preventing School Failure, 57*(4), 181–188.

Heafner, T. T., & Fitchett, P. P. (2015). An opportunity to learn U.S. history: What NAEP data suggest regarding the opportunity gap. *High School Journal, 98*(3), 226–249.

Heinrich, C. J., Darling-Aduana, J., Good, A., & Cheng, H. (Emily). (2019). A look inside online educational settings in high school: Promise and pitfalls for improving educational opportunities and outcomes. *American Educational Research Journal, 56*(6), 2147–2188. https://doi.org/10.3102/0002831219838776

Hood, N. (2020). *Learning from lockdown: What the experiences of teachers, students and parents can tell us about what happened and where to next for New Zealand's school system.* https://theeducationhub.org.nz/wp-content/uploads/2020/08/Learning-from-lockdown.pdf

Hughes, C. A., & Lee, J. Y. (2019). Effective approaches for scheduling and formatting practice: Distributed, cumulative, and interleaved practice. *Teaching Exceptional Children, 51*(6), 411–423.

Hughes, G., Wood, E., & Kitagawa, K. (2014). Use of self-referential (ipsative) feedback to motivate and guide distance learners. *Open Learning, 29*(1), 31–44. https://doi.org/10.1080/02680513.2014.921612

Hunter, R. (2004). *Madeline Hunter's mastery teaching: Increasing instructional effectiveness in elementary and secondary schools.* Corwin.

Isaacs, T., Zara, C., Herbert, G., Coombs, S. J., & Smith, C. (2013). Ipsative assessment. In T. Isaacs, C. Zara, G. Herbert, S. J. Coombs, & C. Smith, *The SAGE key concepts series: Key concepts in educational assessment* (pp. 80–82). SAGE.

Jacka, F. N. (2017). Nutritional psychiatry: Where to next? *EBioMedicine, 17,* 24–29. https://doi.org/10.1016/j.ebiom.2017.02.020

Jenkins, L. (2016). *Optimize your school: It's all about the strategy.* Corwin.

Johnson, E., Mellard, D. F., Fuchs, D., & McKnight, M. A. (2006). *Responsiveness to intervention (RTI): How to do it.* National Research Center on Learning Disabilities. https://files.eric.ed.gov/fulltext/ED496979.pdf

Johnston, P. (2012). *Opening minds: Using language to change lives.* Stenhouse.

Jun, S. W., Ramirez, G., & Cumming, A. (2010). Tutoring adolescents in literacy: A meta-analysis. *McGill Journal of Education, 45*(2), 219–238.

Kirksey, J. J., & Gottfried, M. A. (2018). Familiar faces: Can having similar classmates from last year link to better school attendance this year? *Elementary School Journal, 119*(2), 223–243.

Kraft, M. A., & Falken, G. (2021). *A blueprint for scaling tutoring across public schools* (EdWorkingPaper: 20-335). https://doi.org/10.26300/dkjh-s987

Kuhfeld, M., Soland, J., Tarasawa, B., Johnson, A., Ruzek, E., & Liu, J. (2020a). *Projecting the potential impacts of COVID-19 school closures on academic achievement.* (EdWorkingPaper: 20-226). https://doi.org/10.26300/cdrv-yw05

Kuhfeld, M., Tarasawa, B., Johnson, A., Ruzek, E., & Lewis, K. (2020b). *Learning during COVID-19: Initial findings on students' reading and math achievement and growth.* https://www.nwea.org/content/uploads/2020/11/Collaborative-brief-Learning-during-COVID-19.NOV2020.pdf

Linley, A. (2008). *Average to A+: Realising strengths in yourself and others.* CAPP Press.

Lucile Packard Foundation for Children's Health. (2019). *Ratio of students to pupil support service personnel, by type of personnel.* https://www.kidsdata.org/topic/126/pupil-support-ratio/table

Ma, W., Adesope, O. O., Nesbit, J. C., & Liu, Q. (2014). Intelligent tutoring systems and learning outcomes: A meta-analysis. *Journal of Educational Psychology, 106*(4), 901–918.

Manna, P. (2015). *Developing excellent school principals to advance teaching and learning: Considerations for state policy.* The Wallace Foundation.

Martin, A. J. (2006). Personal bests (PBs): A proposed multidimensional model and empirical analysis. *British Journal of Educational Psychology, 76*(4), 803–825.

Martin, A. J. (2011). Personal best (PB) approaches to academic development: Implications for motivation and assessment. *Educational Practice and Theory, 33*, 93–99.

Marzano, R., & Simms, J. (2013). *Vocabulary for the Common Core.* Marzano Research Lab.

Meckler, L., & Natanson, H. (2020, December 6). "A lost generation": A surge of research reveals students sliding backwards, most vulnerable worst affected. *The Washington Post.* https://www.washingtonpost.com/education/students-falling-behind/2020/12/06/88d7157a-3665-11eb-8d38-6aea1adb3839_story.html

MetLife. (2008). *MetLife survey of the American teacher: The homework experience. A survey of students, teachers and parents.* Author.

Mojtabai, R., Olfson, M., & Han, B. (2016). National trends in the prevalence and treatment of depression in adolescents and young adults. *Pediatrics, 138*, e20161878.

Morales-Chicas, J., & Agger, C. (2017). The effects of teacher collective responsibility on the mathematics achievement of students who repeat algebra. *Journal of Urban Mathematics Education, 10*(1), 52–73.

Muhammad, G. (2020). *Cultivating genius: An equity framework for culturally and historically responsive literacy.* Scholastic.

Mulhearn, G. (2018). *Recognising and acknowledging complexity.* South Australia Department for Education and Child Devlopment. trb.sa.edu.au

Musser, M. P. (2011). *Taking attendance seriously: How school absences undermine student and school performance in New York City.* Campaign for Fiscal Equity.

National Alliance for Mental Illness (NAMI). (2020). *Mental health by the numbers.* https://www.nami.org/mhstats

National Association of State Directors of Special Education. (2005). *Progress monitoring in an RTI model.* https://www.naset.org/fileadmin/user_upload/RTI/RTI_ISSUE__6.pdf

National Research Council. (2012). *Education for life and work: Developing transferable knowledge and skills in the 21st century.* The National Academies Press.

Now Is the Time Technical Assistance Center. (2015). *School mental health referral pathways toolkit.* https://www.escneo.org/Downloads/NITT%20SMHRP%20Toolkit_11%2019%2015%20FINAL.PDF

Nuthall, G. (2007). *The hidden lives of learners.* NZCER Press.

Omoto, A. M., & Packard, C. D. (2016). The power of connections: Psychological sense of community as a predictor of volunteerism. *Journal of Social Psychology, 156*(3), 272–290. https://doi.org/10.1080/00224545.2015.1105777

Palincsar, A., & Brown, A. (1986). Reciprocal teaching of comprehension-fostering and comprehension-monitoring activities. *Cognition and Instruction, 2,* 117–175.

Peña, P. A., & Duckworth, A. L. (2018). The effects of relative and absolute age in the measurement of grit from 9th to 12th grade. *Economics of Education Review, 66,* 183–190. https://doi.org/10.1016/j.econedurev.2018.08.009

Phillips, A., Pane, J. F., Reumann-Moore, R., & Shenbanjo, O. (2020). Implementing an adaptive intelligent tutoring system as an instructional supplement. *Educational Technology Research and Development, 68*(3), 1409–1437.

Pintrich, P. R. (2003). A motivational science perspective on the role of student motivation in learning and teaching contexts. *Journal of Educational Psychology, 95,* 667–686.

Rathore, M. (2019, May 24). *School instructional minutes are not used effectively.* https://thecampanile.org/2019/05/24/school-instructional-minutes-are-not-used-effectively/

Reimers, F. M., & Schleicher, A. (2020). *Schooling disrupted, schooling rethought: How the COVID-19 pandemic is changing education.* https://docplayer.net/187277814-Schooling-disrupted-schooling-rethought.html

Responsive Classroom. (2011). *Closing circle.* https://www.responsiveclassroom.org/closing-circle/

Rickards, F., Hattie, J., & Reid, C. (2020). *The turning point for the teaching profession.* Routledge.

Roediger, H. L., & Karpicke, J. D. (2006). The power of testing memory: Basic research and implications for educational practice. *Perspectives on Psychological Science, 1,* 181–210.

Rosenthal, R., & Jacobson, L. (1992). *Pygmalion in the classroom: Teacher expectation and pupils' intellectual development* (Newly expanded ed.). Crown House Pub.

Rubie-Davies, C. (2008). *Expecting success: Teacher beliefs and practices that enhance student outcomes.* Verlog, Dr. Muller.

Rubie-Davies, C. (2014). *Becoming a high expectation teacher: Raising the bar.* Routledge.

Ruhl, K., & Hughes, C. (2010). *Effective practices for homework. Reading Rockets.* https://www.readingrockets.org/article/effective-practices-homework

Sartain, L. (2004). Foreword. In J. Putzier, *The new normal: Thriving in the age of the individual* (pp. 1–3). Pearson.

Seels, B., & Glasgow, Z. (1997). *Making instructional design decisions* (2nd ed.). Prentice Hall.

Shepherd, S., Owen, D., & Fitch, T. J. (2006). Locus of control and academic achievement in high school students. *Psychological Reports, 98*(2), 318–322. https://doi.org/10.2466/PR0.98.2.318-322

Sherrington, T. (2021). Remote learning solutions: Crowd-sourced ideas for checking students' writing. *Teacherhead.* https://teacherhead.com/2021/01/10/remote-learning-solutions-crowd-sourced-ideas-for-checking-students-writing

Simões, F., & Calheiros, M. M. (2019). A matter of teaching and relationships: determinants of teaching style, interpersonal resources and teacher burnout. *Social Psychology of Education, 22*(4), 991–1013. https://doi.org/10.1007/s11218-019-09501-w

Slavin, R. E., & Lake, C. (2008). Effective programs in elementary mathematics: A best-evidence synthesis. *Review of Educational Research, 78*(3), 427–515. https://doi.org/10.3102/0034654308317473

Smith, D., Fisher, D., & Frey, N. (2015). *Better than carrots or sticks: Restorative practices for positive classroom management.* ASCD.

Sneader, K., & Singhal, S. (2020). *Beyond coronavirus: The path to the next normal.* https://www.mckinsey.com/industries/healthcare-systems-and-services/our-insights/beyond-coronavirus-the-path-to-the-next-normal

Sparks, D., Malkus, N., & Ralph, J. (2015). *Public School Teacher Data File, 2003–04, 2007–08, and 2011–12* (NCES 2015-089). U.S. Department of Education. https://nces.ed.gov/pubs2015/2015089.pdf

Spector, J. M. (2016). *Foundations of educational technology: Integrative approaches and interdisciplinary perspectives.* Routledge.

State Government of Victoria, Australia, Education and Training. (2020). *Lessons learned from Term 2 remote and flexible learning.* https://www.education.vic.gov.au/Documents/about/department/covid-19/lessons-from-term-2-remote-learning.pdf

Templeton, S. (2011). Teaching spelling in the English/language arts classroom. In D. Lapp & D. Fisher (Eds.), *Handbook of research on teaching the English language arts* (3rd ed.). (pp. 247–251). Erlbaum.

Tversky, A., & Kahneman, D. (1974). Judgment under uncertainty: Heuristics and biases. *Science, 185*(4157), 1124–1131.

Valencia, R. R. (n.d.). Deficit thinking paradigm. In J. A. Banks (Ed.), *Encyclopedia of diversity in education.* SAGE. doi:http://dx.doi.org/10.4135/9781452218533.n191

Van der Kolk, B. (2015). *The body keeps the score: Brain, mind, and body in the healing of trauma.* Penguin.

Vaughn, S., Wanzek, J., Linan-Thompson, S., & Murray, C. S. (2007). Monitoring response to supplemental services for students at risk for reading difficulties: High and low responders. In S. R. Jimerson, M. K. Burns, & A. M. VanDerHeyden (Eds.), *Handbook of response to intervention: The science and practice of assessment and intervention* (pp. 234–243). Springer Science & Business Media. doi:10.1007/978-0-387-49053-3_17

Vygotsky, L. S. (1978). *Mind and society: The development of higher mental processes.* Harvard University Press.

Webb, N. (1997). *Research monograph number 6: Criteria for alignment of expectations and assessments on mathematics and science education.* CCSSO. https://www.centralriversaea.org/curriculum/assessment/webbs-depth-knowledge-dok/

Webber, A. (2020). *Using e-asTTle to model short-term learning.* Pepa Mahi, EDK Working Paper, Ministry of Education, New Zealand.

Whitaker, A., Torres-Guillén, S., Morton, M., Jordan, H., Coyle, S., Mann, A., & Sun, W.-L. (2018). *Cops and no counselors: How the lack of school mental health staff is harming students.* https://www.aclu.org/sites/default/files/field_document/030419-acluschooldisciplinereport.pdf

Wiliam, D. (2020). Formative assessment and online teaching. *Australian Institute for Teaching and School Leadership.* Retrieved from https://www.aitsl.edu.au/secondary/comms/australianteacherresponse/formative-assessment-and-online-teaching

Williams, C. (2018, September 19). *Minimizing lost instructional time.* https://www.csas.co/minimizing-lost-instructional-time

Williams, J. L., & Youmans, Q. R. (2020, June 16). *Two pandemics, one responsibility: Constructing a response to COVID-19 and systemic racism.* https://www.acc.org/membership/sections-and-councils/fellows-in-training-section/section-updates/2020/06/12/14/42/two-pandemics-one-responsibility-constructing-a-response-to-covid-19-and-systemic-racism

Woolfolk, A. (2007). *Educational psychology* (10th ed.). Pearson.

Zeiser, K., Scholz, C., & Cirks, V. (2018). *Maximizing student agency: Implementing and measuring student-centered learning practices.* https://files.eric.ed.gov/fulltext/ED592084.pdf

INDEX

ABOUT THE AUTHORS

Douglas Fisher, PhD, is professor and chair of educational leadership at San Diego State University and a leader at Health Sciences High and Middle College, having been an early intervention teacher and elementary school educator. He is the recipient of an International Reading Association William S. Grey citation of merit, an Exemplary Leader award from the Conference on English Leadership of the National Council of Teachers of English, as well as a Christa McAuliffe award for excellence in teacher education. He has published numerous articles on reading and literacy, differentiated instruction, and curriculum design as well as books, such as *PLC+: Better Decisions and Greater Impact by Design, Building Equity*, and *The Distance Learning Playbook*.

Nancy Frey, PhD, is a professor in educational leadership at San Diego State University and a leader at Health Sciences High and Middle College. She has been a special education teacher, reading specialist, and administrator in public schools. Nancy has engaged in professional learning communities as a member and in designing schoolwide systems to improve teaching and learning for all students. She has published numerous books, including *The Teacher Clarity Playbook* and *The Distance Learning Playbook.*

Dominique Smith, EdD, is a social worker, school administrator, mentor, national trainer for the International Institute on Restorative Practices, and member of Corwin's Visible Learning for Literacy Cadre. He is passionate about creating school cultures that honor students and build their confidence and competence. He is the winner of the National School Safety Award from the School Safety Advocacy Council. Dominique's major area of research and instruction focuses on restorative practices, classroom management, growth mindset, and the culture of achievement. He earned his master's degree in social work from the University of Southern California and his doctoral degree in educational leadership at San Diego State University.

John Hattie, PhD, is an award-winning education researcher and best-selling author with nearly 30 years of experience examining what works best in student learning and achievement. His research, better known as Visible Learning, is a culmination of nearly 30 years synthesizing more than 1,500 meta-analyses comprising more than 90,000 studies involving over 300 million students around the world. He has presented and keynoted in over 350 international conferences and has received numerous recognitions for his contributions to education. His notable publications include *Visible Learning*, *Visible Learning for Teachers*, *Visible Learning and the Science of How We Learn*, *Visible Learning for Mathematics, Grades K–12,* and, most recently, *10 Mindframes for Visible Learning*.

A SAGE Publishing Company

The PLC+ Books

Corwin's PLC+ framework is aimed at refreshing current collaborative structures and helps support teachers' decision making in the context of individual and collective efficacy, expectations, equity, and the activation of their own learning. The PLC+ books provide a foundation for this critical work.

PLC+

Better Decisions and Greater Impact by Design

What's this book about?

- Provides a brief history of PLCs
- Introduces the PLC+ framework questions and crosscutting themes
- Shows the PLC+ in action in various settings

When do I need this book?

- You want to understand the purpose of PLCs
- You want to learn a new framework for effective PLCs
- You want to reinvigorate and increase the impact of your existing PLC

The PLC+ Playbook

A Hands-On Guide to Collectively Improving Student Learning

What's this book about?

- Provides a practical, hands-on guide to implementing the full PLC+ cycle
- Guides PLC+ group members through 22 modules as they answer the five guiding questions and focus on the four crosscutting themes
- Offers modules comprising an array of tools that support implementation of the PLC+ framework

When do I need this book?

- You want to plan and implement the PLC+ framework in collaborative settings
- You want to implement the PLC+ model step by step in your own PLC

The PLC+ Activator's Guide

What's this book about?

- Provides guidance for the PLC+ team activators

When do I need this book?

- You are a PLC+ activator and want to do the best possible job for your group
- You are an activator and want to pre-plan the implementation of your PLC+
- You need help to guide the group in overcoming obstacles or having difficult conversations

PLCN21241